The Chiricahua Mountains

The
Chiricahua
Mountains

formerly: Sky Island

Weldon F. Heald
Drawings by C. M. Palmer, Jr.

The University of Arizona Press
Tucson, Arizona

About the Author . . .

WELDON FAIRBANKS HEALD spent several of the last years of his life in
the Chiricahua Mountains in southeastern Arizona, where he continued
his intense appreciation of nature. An authority on the flora, fauna,
history, climate, and geographic wonders of the eleven western states,
he held offices in the American Alpine Club, Sierra Club, and Explorers
Club, and membership in many other conservation organizations.
In 1961 he acted as Consultant on National Parks and Monuments
under the Secretary of the Interior. Heald's numerous published works
include countless journal articles, scenic guides to five of the western
states, and books (on which he collaborated) entitled *The Sierra
Nevada: Range of Light, High Sierra: Mountain Wonderland,* and
The Inverted Mountains: Canyons of the West. Heald Peak, a majestic
mountain overlooking Lake Isabella in Sequoia National Forest, in
April 1974 was dedicated to Heald by a group of Sierra Club members.

Acknowledgment is made to the U.S. Department of the
Interior, Fish and Wildlife Service, for photographs used
on pages 55 and 70, and to Ray Manley for the cover
and title page photographs. All other photographs are by
the author.

Fourth printing 1984
THE UNIVERSITY OF ARIZONA PRESS

ISBN 0-8165-0491-1
L. C. No. 75-12070

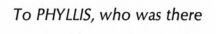

To PHYLLIS, who was there

Contents

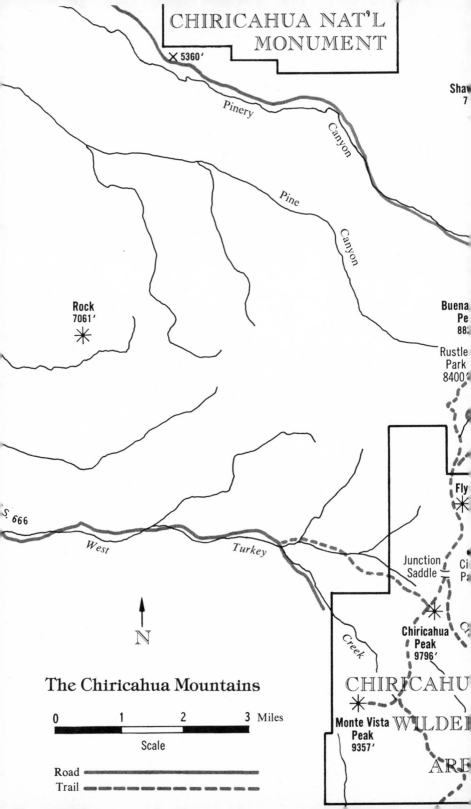

CHIRICAHUA NAT'L
MONUMENT

✕ 5360'

Pinery

Canyon

Shaw
7

Pine

Canyon

Rock
7061'
✳

Buena
Pe
88.

Rustle
Park
8400'

S. 666

Fly
✳

West

Turkey

Junction
Saddle

Ci
Pa

✳

↑
N

Creek

Chiricahua
Peak
9796'

CHIRICAHU

The Chiricahua Mountains

✳
Monte Vista
Peak
9357'

WILDE

ARE

0   1   2   3 Miles

Scale

Road
Trail

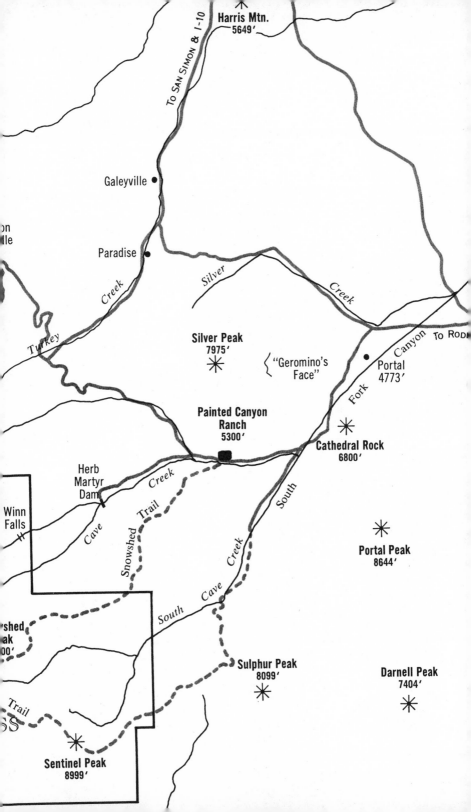

Introduction

There are islands in the desert as well as in the sea. No one recognizes the fact better than Weldon F. Heald, author of this fine book. He has lived on and near the desert islands of southern Arizona for many years and knows them intimately.

These "islands" are mountain ranges that rise from the arid Sonoran Desert lands of the American Southwest to heights of fir-clad coolness. At their bases mesquite trees offer faint shade from the 110-degree temperature of a summer day. Most animals and reptiles wait patiently in hidden burrows for evening, while, a vertical mile above, moist-nosed black bears romp among the pines in a comfortable 72 degrees. It is a country of amazing contrasts.

Weldon Heald has traversed these mountains afoot and on horseback every season of the year, written about them, and photographed them. More than that he has lived in them, and the story of *Sky Island* is about his years in the wildest and most fascinating of all—the Chiricahua Mountains.

This is a genial volume of wonderful places and of life, both human and animal, with no over-emphasis on either. The hard-fighting Apache Indians once defended the rugged mountains almost to their last drop of blood, some of which, even after all these years, spills over onto several pages of this book. There are tales, too, of pioneers, cattlemen, miners, ghost towns, and buried treasure. The Healds, Weldon and Phyllis, are both authors of note. Weldon's highly professional skill shines forth as his narrative progresses. Some of his descriptions are unforgettable. Many of his phrases are of the type that the reader ponders and thinks, "I wish I had said that."

During the time the Healds lived at their Chiricahua Painted Canyon Ranch they were hosts to friends from all over the country and literally hundreds of strangers from thirty-seven states and eight foreign countries. Animal visitors were also always welcome. Birds of a surprising number and variety, bears, mountain lions, coyotes, and a stray wolf or two, which had probably wandered over from nearby Old Mexico, enjoyed the safety and security of the Heald's ranch. There, they never found a gun pointed at them.

The Healds are sincere conservationists who have always practised what they preach. This fact is frequently apparent with telling effect in *Sky Island*. Weldon Heald is a strong advocate of preserving some of our magnificent scenic wilderness heritage while there is still time. But he is never strident and seldom controversial.

In this book there is flavor and substance as well as good sound philosophy of the kind not discovered in college courses. If I seem prejudiced, it's because I am. I love these desert islands, too. There has never been enough written about them. We are fortunate, in this instance, that one of them has found such an excellent chronicler.

William H. Carr
Founder and Director Emeritus, Arizona-Sonora Desert Museum.
Vice President, Charles Lathrop Pack Forestry Foundation.

Tucson, Arizona

The Chiricahua Mountains

1 Going Home

From the copper-smelting town of Douglas, transcontinental Highway 80 angles up across the extreme southeastern corner of Arizona into New Mexico. Phyllis and I must have driven it back and forth a hundred times, for this was the most direct route between our Painted Canyon Ranch and the nearest shopping center, sixty-five miles distant.

Douglas lies close against the Mexican border fence in broad, treeless Sulphur Spring Valley. Outlanders might call it desert country, but Arizonans know better. An elevation of 4,000 feet gives enough precipitation to spread the valley with miles and miles of grass. In fact, it's prime cattle range, and here and there artesian wells spill water over the fertile soil in a checkerboard of green, irrigated farmlands. But Douglas's population of fifteen thousand makes it the metropolis of southeastern Arizona, and to us this was as urban as we liked to get.

After loading the station wagon with groceries, dog food, a gallon of Mexican rum, baling wire, typewriter ribbons, and anything else we or the ranch needed, Phyllis and I would head out of Douglas on Highway 80, bound for home. The town has no cluttering suburbs, and the road slants up the long east slope of the valley, passes under the pink granite ramparts of the College Peaks, crosses the height of land, then gently descends into San Bernardino Valley. This is the next wide inter-mountain trough to the east, and changes its name northward to San Simon Valley. The road follows the flat, level floor for forty miles, with never an eccentric jog or swing.

Here we breathed deeper and squinted our eyes like old-timers in the brilliant Southwestern sunshine. The twin white plumes of smoke from the Douglas smelter were gone, and we looked over

a slice of Arizona much as it was in pioneer days. Cattle ranches, big as counties in the East, lie across the valley between mountain borders fifteen miles apart. Grazing Herefords and Brahmas dot the grassy expanse, and groups of them are usually gathered at watering places by the occasional steel windmills. Signs of human occupation are mostly limited to far-away ranch houses and buildings at the entrances to mountain canyons.

Phyllis and I have a fondness for these windmills which stand like exclamation points in the empty landscape. We often stopped at one near the road, just to listen. No sound is more fundamentally Western than the *clank-clank-clank* of a windmill, and each one has a distinctive wheeze, squeak, or rattle of its own. If life were longer, I would make tape recordings of windmills. Then, played back anywhere, I'd be transported in imagination to the far-flung open range of the Southwest under its vast, arching blue sky.

This part of Arizona, southern New Mexico, and down into Mexico was once the territory of the savage and warlike Apache Indians. For two centuries they fiercely fought for their homeland, and no white man, woman, or child was safe from their depredations. Like devastating tornadoes, mounted bands of Apache war-

San Bernardino Valley, Arizona.

riors suddenly swooped down on settlements, ranches, wagon trains, and stagecoaches in whirlwinds of pillage, destruction, and sudden death, then as quickly retired to their mountain strongholds. Even the U. S. Army was baffled and helpless against the quicksilver strategy of the wily Apaches. These red-skinned adversaries were mobile needles in a giant haystack.

Beside the highway, forty miles from Douglas, stands a masonry pillar about twenty-five feet high. Called the Geronimo Surrender Monument, it commemorates the final capture of the last battling Apache chief by army forces in 1886. The actual capitulation took place in Skeleton Canyon, a few miles southeast in New Mexico. Geronimo had made peace several times before but always jumped the reservation and went on the warpath again. Nobody had a good word to say about this Indian. He was treacherous, cruel, crafty, and apparently without human feelings. But then, no Apache had a good word to say about white men either. They were treacherous, cruel, crafty, and spoke with "forked tongues." However, the entire Southwest breathed easier when Geronimo and his braves were herded on a train bound for resettlement in Florida. His surrender marked the end of the pioneer period and the beginning of modern times.

A little boy who visited us with his family was asked by his grandfather when he returned East: "Did you see any Indians?"

"How could I?" he answered scornfully. "They didn't have a TV set at the ranch."

It's true that the Apache heritage in Arizona's southeastern corner is meager. It consists of a few isolated mountain gravestones inscribed "Killed by Indians," arrowheads marking ancient battlegrounds, and assorted relics scattered around the Indians' favorite camp sites. But the former inhabitants are well-remembered in place names. For instance, beyond the Geronimo monument the Chiricahua Mountains, once a formidable natural fortress of the Chiricahua Apache tribe, stretch northward, bordering the valley on the west. Their rugged flanks, rising a vertical mile against the sky, are scarred with cliffs and broken by narrow canyons that reach back to a row of dark evergreen-forested summits. Pronounced *chee-ree-cah'-wah*, the range is familiarly known to almost everybody roundabout as the "Cheery Cows." In Apache language Chiricahua means "Big Mountain" or "Wild Turkey." Experts disagree. I incline toward the latter translation because south in Mexico the Tarahumares call the turkey *chee-wee-kee* or *chee-ree-kee*, and these cave-dwelling Indians in former times had close association with the Apaches—mostly violent and bloody.

About fifty miles from Douglas we would cross the line into New Mexico, passing a big sign that always welcomed us to the "Land of Enchantment." Then comes Rodeo, the only sizable settlement on the entire drive. If Rodeo were more Western, it would have to be moved out into the Pacific. The place resembles a frontier movie set, and one can visualize a grim Marshall Dillon issuing from between the swinging doors of the Long Branch to outdraw a killer in the middle of the street. Rodeo has no saloons now, only taverns with recorded a-go-go background music. That's how effete the Old West has become. The town's attractions aren't immediately apparent to the hurrying passer-by. But loyalties are staunch and tenacious in these parts, and we know a Rodeo lady who was so homesick at her daughter's in California that she returned to live out her days, never more to stray.

4

Windmills stand like exclamation points in the empty landscape.

Highway 80 sweeps on to El Paso, Forth Worth, and Dallas, and the persistent motorist can eventually wet his front wheels in the Atlantic at Savannah, Georgia. But our way home was the left-hand turn to Portal, three miles beyond Rodeo. This side road crosses back into Arizona and aims straight for the great mass of the Chiricahuas, seven miles distant. It traverses an arid stretch of valley scattered with low creosote bushes, and enlivened by leaping, long-eared jackrabbits and scurrying lizards. Phyllis and I once saw a lethargic, black-and-orange gila monster here but, as a rule, Arizona's only poisonous lizard prefers the low, hot desert country west of the highlands. We estimated he was two feet long from snout to tip of his fat, overstuffed tail, but we didn't measure him with scientific exactitude.

The first indication of different things to come is tree-lined Cave Creek where it escapes from the confines of the mountains. Unlike the sweet Afton, Cave Creek at this point neither flows gently nor very often. It can be a roaring, coffee-colored flood as after summer cloudbursts, or its bed can be bone-dry for months. But with normal precipitation or better in the lofty headwaters, Cave Creek is a delightful, singing stream, cascading and swirling down

Fresh snow on the high Chiricahuas.

through a green tunnel of big, arching sycamores, cottonwoods, walnuts, and willows.

Crossing the bridge over the creek, Phyllis and I would drive into Portal and draw up in front of the post office. We hoped for news from the busy outside world, and maybe a check or two from kindly-disposed editors. Although Painted Canyon Ranch was five miles farther, amidst the jumbled Chiricahuas, we were now on our own stamping grounds. Portal was our address, and we considered ourselves Portalites.

With time, every foot of the drive between Douglas and Portal became familiar. We knew the exact spot where we changed a tire at 1:30 A.M. after a party in town; the place the Texas couple with the baby ran out of gas fifteen miles from the nearest service station; and the point where the station wagon went dead for no reason we could discover. After being towed to Rodeo and later receiving a goodly repair bill, I believe the garageman told us the finnegan pin jammed, closing the fluter valve. I can't be sure now. But these memories, and many more, enlivened the road, giving us a sense of intimate association closely akin to ownership.

We traveled the route all seasons in every kind of weather. We saw flaming sunsets, and the silver cast of full-moonlight over the valley. There were gray days and golden days—blinding sunshine and slashing rain. In spring the way was ribboned with blue lupines, and masses of goldpoppies mottled the landscape with bright orange-yellow patterns. Later the yuccas raised their spikes of creamy-white blossoms. In midsummer high-piled thunder clouds stabbed the hills with lightning and trailed opaque curtains of rain over the land. Then, refreshed, the valley would spread a carpet of grass, green and lush as the Vermont countryside. But there was exhilaration, too, in winter when the sere, brown valley was backed by mountains glittering with freshly fallen snow.

On almost every trip cocky roadrunners dashed across the highway in front of us, raised their wings, and glided to safety on the other side. Special symbol of the Southwest, this off-beat relative of the cuckoo is famous for its victorious battles with rattlesnakes. But recently the racing roadrunner gained eminence in human affairs when it was chosen as state bird of New Mexico and as em-

The rocky entrance to Cave Creek Canyon.

blem of Governor Sam's "Go With Goddard!" gubernatorial campaign.

Lean coyotes trotted unafraid by the roadside, sometimes standing to watch us pass, then suddenly vanishing in the sparse brush. And once we spotted a husky Mexican lobo wolf, probably on a visit from across the border. This corner of Arizona and adjacent New Mexico is one of the four widely separated areas in the United States, south of Alaska, where the rapidly diminishing race of gray wolves fight for survival. Then we stopped one time to allow a slow-poke desert tortoise to clear the road, and occasionally paused for softly clucking mama and papa quail leading their covey of youngsters. Flying, running, hopping, and crawling life spiced our trips. But, strangely enough, neither of us can recall seeing a snake on our drives to Douglas and back.

As its names implies, Portal is a gateway to the mountains, with the impressive, rock-guarded entrance to Cave Creek Canyon just beyond. Aptly christened around the turn of the century by its prospector-founder, Portal's pronunciation is English, not accented on the second syllable the Spanish way.* The community consists of a handful of houses along the creek, a third-class post office, one-room school, and grocery store fronted by twin gasoline pumps—regular and super.

But Portal, though hardly a town, is a center of valley and highland people for miles around, at least a couple of hundred altogether. Because of the superior brand of climate and scenery, the vicinity has developed in recent years as a country residential retreat with resort overtones. Easterners have bought ranches and fruit orchards, a few new homes grace scenic hilltops and canyon sites, while cabins and a couple of rustic lodges furnish limited accommodations for vacationists who have discovered the hidden delights of the Chiricahuas.

Portal even boasts a small museum, a white-painted adobe pueblo-style building in which fragments of the past are respectfully preserved. Here are Indian pots, baskets, and ornaments, and the more civilized white men's artifacts, such as whiskey bot-

---

* Phyllis and I are sensitive about pronunciations because we are almost invariably called *Held* on the first try. The proper pronunciation is *Heeld*.

tles and sardine tins from the once-active nearby mining camp of Paradise and the long-gone outlaw hangout called Galeyville. These treasures may be seen by borrowing the museum key at the AVA Ranch, a half-mile north of town.

The most interesting exhibit to me is the stuffed jaguar. He was shot in 1912, the last of his kind to be seen in the Chiricahuas. Sometimes weighing as much as two hundred and fifty pounds, tawny, black-spotted "El Tigre" is runner-up cat to the lion and tiger in size but bows to none other in strength and agility. The jaguar ranges from Argentina to Mexico and once strayed as far north as Arkansas and Colorado. No more magnificent exemplar of wild America exists, but instant death is the penalty for crossing the line into the Land of the Free and Home of the Brave. As a result, jaguars are becoming increasingly scarce, and only three have been killed in southern Arizona during the past six years. However, shooting "El Tigre" is presumably such sport that local professional hunters have conducted safaris to Venezuela where he still reigns as king of the jungle.

After picking up the mail and glancing at the bills, Phyllis and I would then point the car toward the gigantic slot of Cave Creek Canyon. This last lap to the ranch was on the little road that winds and twists for twenty-two miles over the high backbone of the range and drops down the western slope to Sulphur Spring Valley. Now came the buoyant, lightly anticipatory feeling I always have on going into the mountains. Lowland problems are left behind, and the world seems fresher and less complicated. First we passed the sign reading "Entering Coronado National Forest," next the former Portal Ranger Station, now leased as a private residence, then the sky-reaching walls of the canyon closed in upon us.

The way threads the wooded depths beside the musical stream. Above on either side tower sheer cliffs, topped by crenellated battlements and groups of slender columns, while yawning caves, arches, and windows have been carved into the stone by centuries of wind, rain, frost, and melted snow. The rock, called latite, is of volcanic origin and glows with soft shades of orange, pink, yellow, and deep salmon as if it had been daubed by a giant paint-

*The walls of Cave Creek Canyon rise sheer
above the Chiricahua Mountain Road.*

brush. The most striking single feature is Cathedral Rock, a massive monolithic wedge on the east wall, 2,000 feet high. The canyon floor is pleasantly sylvan, with oaks, sycamores, pines, and junipers shading a tangled under-story of greenery almost as luxuriant as the tropics, after generous summer rains.

Beyond the left-hand South Fork branch of Cave Creek, the canyon bends to the west toward the main divide of the Chirica-

huas. In a mile or so more the steep walls draw back and the road suddenly enters a roomy interior basin with the high silhouette of the main divide straight ahead. Right here was our Painted Canyon Ranch. We passed the pool, the tree-studded lawn, and drew up to the gate beyond the house. Behind it was "Beautiful," front paws on a rail, yelping and waving her graceful collie tail in greeting. Beside her were "Barney," "Pinky," and "White Christmas"—"Whitey" for short—displaying their own more quiet feline welcome. The trip to town and back was over.

We were home.

Cathedral Rock towers 2,000 feet over Cave Creek Canyon.

2 *Mountain Islanders*

Our ranch was unique—at least we had never seen anything like it before. It combined nature and civilization in perfect proportions. But Phyllis and I were by no means the first to discover this secluded Elysium in the Chiricahua Mountains. It was originally homesteaded by Stephan Reed in 1879. He was a tough Missourian who joined the California Gold Rush and passed through southern Arizona on his way West. The country exerted a magnetic fascination on the young pioneer, as it does on a lot of us today. Stephan Reed didn't forget, and, after twenty years as a miner and farmer in the Mother Lode, he returned to Arizona with his family. The Chiricahuas were his choice. He built the first wagon road up the canyon to this spot on Cave Creek where he planted an apple orchard and vegetable patch, raised cattle, horses, hogs, and poultry, and lived peacefully in his wilderness home for thirty-two years.

Across the meadow the Reed cabin still stands, shaded by a spreading walnut tree. Constructed of squared pine logs, hand-split shakes, and whip-sawed floor boards, it is probably the oldest house in the southeastern part of the state. We inherited the historic structure in a dilapidated, run-down condition and made a project of restoring it to make it livable. The stone fireplace and chimney were rebuilt, leaks in the roof repaired, rotting timbers replaced, and running water, a bathtub, and flush toilet installed —luxuries the Reeds never enjoyed. We even talked of setting a plaque in the wall reading "Geronimo Slept Here," but never got around to it.

However, such a reminder of the past would have testified to the remarkable character of Stephan Reed. He must have been an exceptionally warm and personable human being. Around him on all sides whites were shot, clubbed to death, and tortured by Indians, but neither Reed nor his family were molested, and he was never forced to raise a gun in self-defense. Yet each fall he drove his cattle to the railroad, thirty-five miles north, and took wagon-loads of big red apples and farm produce through Apache-infested country to the mining camp of Silver City, over in New Mexico. He also sold meat and vegetables in hard-bitten Galeyville, five miles north on Turkey Creek, and had no trouble with Curley Bill, John Ringo, Johnny-Behind-the-Deuce, or other gun-toting rustlers and smugglers hiding out from the law. Most surprising of all, Stephan Reed was presumably the only white man in the Territory on friendly terms with Geronimo. The story goes that the malevolent Apache chief often visited the cabin and sometimes camped with his braves at the Reed place.

The patriarch of Painted Canyon Ranch died in 1912 at the age of eighty-three and is buried in a little fenced-in plot among the Chihuahua pines and oaks across Cave Creek. Besides Reed's headstone, there are four others: Isabel Reed, his second wife; Leslie, his eldest son; Alf Hands, a neighbor killed by Indians; and the infant daughter of family friends named Wolfe.

The old Reed Cabin.

Other owners of the ranch came and went, until the 1930's when the property was purchased by a copper company executive from Douglas. He built the present main house as a week-end and summer home and planned a baronial mansion at the edge of the meadow for his retirement. We found the architect's drawings on a closet shelf and estimated that this stone dream castle would have cost at least seventy-five thousand dollars. But the plans were never completed, because both he and his son were killed by lightning.

Added to and modernized by subsequent owners, the main house when we bought it was a rambling, comfortable sort of place with no architectural pretensions whatever. The exterior was white painted wood siding with long sloping roofs and wide verandas, while inside were big, high-ceilinged rooms and a fieldstone fireplace large enough to take four-foot logs. A year or so before our time a dude ranch was contemplated and two separate cottages were erected. Although the idea was a good one, it never materialized, and Phyllis and I used one cottage as a guest house and converted the other into twin studies. These workrooms became hives of mental industry, as the principal reason we quit livestock raising and moved to Painted Canyon Ranch was to devote full time to writing.

All around us were trees, grass, running streams, and meadows bright with summer wildflowers—a setting reminiscent of New England rather than down near the Mexican border. The front lawn sloped from the house a couple of hundred feet to a swimming pool fed by a constant warm spring with a year-round temperature of seventy-two degrees. Cold springs, too, bubbled up here and there among beds of watercress, a ribbon-like cascade laced a distant cliff, and a deep backwater in Cave Creek was the home of a family of rainbow trout, ranging from six inches to over a foot in length. I never mentioned our half-dozen trusting fish because a determined angler could have eliminated them in half an hour. But I often visited them and sat on a rock beside a miniature waterfall watching their effortless turns, rolls, dives, and lightning-like strikes as they surfaced to take the pieces of bread I threw them. Alas, Nature not man was their nemesis. One summer

Painted Canyon Ranch.

a flash flood swept down the creek and filled the pools with silt and mud, burying the fish. Possibly they will be preserved for posterity by being fossilized for some future paleontologist to puzzle over.

What Phyllis and I liked best about the place were our reserved front seats at some of Nature's grandest shows. We could watch winter storms sweep over the divide and drape the peaks in dazzling white; listen to the reverberating crash of summer thunder and hear the roar of the oncoming rain; enjoy the flaming reds, yellows, orange, and russet of autumn foliage; and see the landscape come to life each spring in brave new greenery. And always we could pass the time of day with the wild turkeys, peccaries, coatis, deer, and a host of other animals and birds who owned the Painted Canyon Ranch, too.

For where we lived practically the whole parade of North Amer-

Guest house and studies at Painted Canyon Ranch.

ica's natural world passed by sooner or later. In fact, the Chiricahuas contain a greater concentration, a wider variation of wildlife, vegetation, and climatic conditions than any other area of similar size in the United States. The difference in climate between the arid, cactus-studded outer slopes and the dense coniferous forests on top is as great as one would encounter on a 2,000-mile trip north to Canada's Hudson Bay. Between the two extremes mammals, birds, reptiles, insects, and plants typical of the Rockies, Pacific Coast, and Mexico meet and mingle with local varieties found nowhere else. One collector counted 507 species of plants from eighty botanical families in a small section of the Chiricahuas, and an ornithologist with 470 different birds on his lifetime list spotted fifty-seven species new to him on a five-day visit.

These mountains are one of a dozen or so isolated ranges that rise abruptly from the broad desert basins and grassy upland valleys of southeastern Arizona. Although second in altitude to the Pinalenos, sixty miles to the northwest, they are the most extensive and complex of them all. Standing like a great wall between San Simon and Sulphur Spring valleys, the Chiricahuas stretch north and south for forty miles, have a maximum width of twenty miles, and culminate in a skyline of rounded summits between nine and ten thousand feet high. The range is a scrambled geological hodge-podge of granite, gneiss, sandstone, limestone, shale, and ancient lava flows which have been eroded through the ages into a maze of deep, plunging canyons, soaring precipices, pinnacles, sharp ridges, and fantastic rock formations. I know of no other mountains in the Southwest that can match the Chiricahuas in sheer number of impressive scenic features—but maybe prejudice disqualifies me as a competent judge.

These widely scattered southern Arizona ranges are literally islands in the sky. Although separated by land instead of water, the ranges stand apart, as different from their surroundings as if they rose from some remote sea. There are, of course, similar family characteristics but each has a distinctive personality of its own. In this way they resemble islands of a group, such as the Azores or Hawaii.

The feeling of insularity is very real. Phyllis and I were as much islanders at Painted Canyon Ranch as when we wrote a play one winter on Oahu's Kanaha Bay. Detached from the busyness and turmoil of human affairs, we tended to identify ourselves closely with the Chiricahuas and to refer to the rest of the world as "Outside." But, above all, we found life there calmer, the tempo slower, and today's problems less pressing. Perhaps that is because we could view them more dispassionately and in truer perspective, as they seldom affected us personally. At any rate, we are convinced that a mountain island is a way of life as well as a place to live.

It would be a mistake to assume that the Chiricahuas are a lingering pocket of hillbilly culture, like Mount Idy or Grinders Switch. History, folklore, and background are regional, but the inhabitants retain few frontier customs. The country around them plays a dominating role in the people's lives. They are a part of it —it is a part of them. But the nation-wide tide of restless humanity is diluting the rugged, back-country independence they inherited from the pioneers. The first time I climbed the steel tower atop 9,666-foot Flys Peak the lookout was chuckling over

A setting reminiscent of New England.

The New Yorker, and we had a two-hour discussion about modern literature in his little glass-enclosed house with most of southern Arizona spread out below us. He was much better informed on the subject than I was.

A year or so after Phyllis and I arrived we all joined a Rural Electrification Administration cooperative, thereby incurring a whopping communal debt of two million dollars. The 220-volt power made our individual motor-driven electric plants obsolete and put deep freezes, refrigerators, washing machines, hair dryers, and other appliances in the farthest mountain ranch houses and cabins. Then, too, the efficient wires of the telephone company now replace the wheezy, unpredictable Forest Service lines which once wandered informally from tree to tree up the canyon and over the divide. In those days the phones went dead after nearly every storm, and even when they worked a pertinent greeting would have been, "I don't know who you are or what you're saying, but it's good to hear your voice." However, television waves cannot penetrate the Chiricahuas' rocky fastnesses, so Ed Sullivan and

The Man from U.N.C.L.E. still remain legendary national heroes.

As a matter of fact, living in a sky island taught us that the greatest stronghold of ingrained provincialism is the populous, cosmopolitan East Coast. One time I wrote an article titled "A Paean to Cheese" for New York's graciously suave *Gourmet* magazine. In accepting the manuscript, the editors made no mention of its mellifluous prose, but were wide-eyed with wonder that anyone from a place called Portal way out in Arizona would be cognizant of the cheese situation at the international level. Again, a super-sophisticated novelist and his wife rented the Barker sisters'

A quiet backwater in Cave Creek Canyon.

charming adobe home. He wanted undisturbed quiet for writing his third best-seller. On entering the living room for the first time he looked around and remarked with patronizing geniality, "My, you're quite civilized here, aren't you?"

He was correct. The Barker sisters are two of the most civilized persons we've met in many a year. Native southeastern Arizonans, they've written two successful juvenile books and conducted a children's boarding school. One was the first woman State Superintendent of Schools and ex-officio member of the Parole Board, while the other is an accomplished painter and was a well-known professional puppeteer who toured the Far Western states with shows which she wrote herself. The Barker sisters' interests are wide-ranging and their conversation is spiced with wit and spirit. The novelist labored at his typewriter and spent his leisure time in lepidopteral pursuits with a big butterfly net, until his wife saw a snake. The next day they packed up and hastily retreated to their Manhattan apartment high above snakeless but far more dangerous Central Park. Which reminds me that Phyllis and I

Winter storm clearing, from our reserved front seats.

didn't use a key or lock a door during the time we lived at Painted Canyon Ranch.

In the mountains beyond us were a dozen Forest Service lease summer cabins and a Boy Scout camp at Rustler Park near the top of the divide. But our nearest year-round neighbors to the west lived seventeen miles distant via the little road that climbs over the Chiricahuas and down the other side. However, we acquired new neighbors on the east a couple of years after we arrived. They were Bill and Mrs. Hoskins who built a home in an opening among the oaks and pines on Cave Creek a half-mile below us. Bill was an army Lieutenant Colonel retired on disability who married a Chiricahua girl and ran a general store in Portal until they moved up the canyon next door to us. Life was pleasanter after they came, for the Hoskins followed a good neighbor policy beyond the line of duty. About the only return we could make for their many kindnesses was to pick up their mail on our daily, ten-mile round trip to the post office and leave it in a homemade box beside the road near the Hoskins' house. More often than not we'd find in it one of Mrs. Hoskins' famous fruit pies, a mess of trout, chili beans, or a jug of cider. So on balance the Colonel and his Lady stayed well ahead of us.

At the age of eight I had been introduced to the mountains. We immediately struck up an acquaintance that developed into a lifelong friendship and, like California's naturalist John Muir, I became "forever and hopelessly a mountaineer." For much of my life I have lived within sight of mountains, at their feet or on their lower slopes. But there was never any sense of belonging. That is, until one night on the topmost pinnacle of Silver Peak in the Chiricahuas. As the sun set and a score of white-throated swifts and violet-green swallows played tag in the air around me, the mountains and valleys changed color and darkened into the deep purple of twilight. Suddenly the faint hum of a distant motor came up from the south. I looked down and saw a pinpoint of light 2,600 feet directly below. Phyllis had turned on the electricity at Painted Canyon Ranch and that was the sound of our power plant.

"So," I thought, "this is no longer some remote, lonely, distant spot. This is my backyard!"

This is my backyard!

3 Escape

Phyllis and I were refugees from the smog and ever-increasing congestion of Southern California. For fifteen years we had a home on six slanting acres up against the Sierra Madre range which looked out over the great level spread of the San Gabriel Valley. Below us was Pasadena and, beyond, the vast urban sprawl of Los Angeles stretched to the Pacific. With field glasses we could see the warships in Long Beach Harbor, thirty miles away.

When Phyllis and I built our house the environment was pleasantly semi-rural, and we intended to spend the rest of our lives there. Across the little canyon to the east was undeveloped hillside property, mostly chaparral, belonging to the famous Western novelist, Zane Grey. He planned to fence several hundred acres and stock the place with exotic African animals. But he died, the land was sold, and instead of zebras and wart hogs for neighbors, we got people—hundreds of them. Within a short time crowded subdivisions hemmed us in on all sides, and the gray-white blanket of smog rolled up from the city about 10:00 A.M., blotting out the view for the rest of the day. More often than not we couldn't even see the mountains close behind us. Phyllis and I coughed, our eyes watered, and we tried to get used to the acrid smell of human progress.

One evening as we sat on the patio looking into the impenetrable man-made murk, involuntary listeners to the blare of a new neighbor's television entertainment, we suddenly decided we had had enough. Phyllis brought me the afternoon paper and pointed to a classified advertisement listing an 8,000 acre cattle ranch for sale in Arizona's southeastern corner. We didn't know anything about raising cattle, but the ad said an expert cowman went with the place and we figured we could learn.

26

A few days later we drove to Arizona, looked the ranch over for three hours, and bought it. Fortunately, the demand for Southern California foothill real estate enabled us to sell out with a good profit. So we started life as cattle ranchers with a little extra money in the bank.

We needed it!

"They say cows work for you while you sleep," said Phyllis optimistically.

But we soon found sleep to be a luxury. When the livestock didn't need attention, the ranch did. It required twelve to sixteen hours a day just to keep things even. There was branding and doctoring, herding and supplemental feeding, painting, fence-repairing, machine-tinkering, and well-digging, together with a never-ending round of ranch chores. In fact, we discovered the hard way that one should begin learning the cattle business at the age of four—even earlier would be preferable. And I recommend a stout constitution.

Our California and Eastern friends were interested in the venture. One asked: "How do you pass the time on a ranch? For instance, what do you do after breakfast?"

"We take a break and watch the sunrise," said Phyllis.

Two things about operating a working ranch are basic. First, unless you're a millionaire, don't go fancy. Like a thirsty sponge absorbing water, a ranch will take any amount of money you pour into it and yet never be anywhere near finished. Secondly, if you have a cattle spread, keep it strictly a cattle spread. Being green newcomers, Phyllis and I didn't. Besides the original beef on the hoof and the necessary horses, we added dairy cows, chickens, turkeys, ducks, pigs, and rabbits. We even took a flyer in bullfrogs.

The prospectus promised enormous profits and we ordered a pair of pedigreed croakers from Arkansas at twenty-five dollars apiece. A couple of weeks later two ventilated boxes arrived, with the huge amphibians nestled inside in beds of wet moss. Cecil, our inherited cowman, and I deposited them in a specially prepared enclosure with water rights in a spring-fed pond a half-mile back of the house. Although we later searched diligently for them, and almost dragged the pond, we never saw the frogs again. I sus-

There was branding . . .

pected a five-foot gopher snake who lived nearby but was never able to prove anything. Phyllis and I missed the one hundred and fifty thousand dollars those frogs and their progeny would have made us in three years.

We named our outfit the Flying H Ranch and had a registered brand which looked like this ⊬. Both Phyllis and I look back on our active cattle-ranching as one of the most rewarding experiences in our lives. We found that we had escaped to a deeper and more fundamental reality than seems to prevail in the crowded, sophisticated centers of human activity. There Man is insulated by his own rigid communal shell and has lost contact with Nature, which gave him birth.

Out under the brilliant Arizona sun, with a hundred-mile

sweep of country for a background, people are still important, but they fail to remain individually impressive. Nature quickly whittles them down to size. This is perhaps why class distinctions are practically non-existent and a man is never rated by his business or position. He stands or falls by what he is, not what he has. At rural parties and community gatherings everyone from cooks and cow punchers to prospectors, dudes, and tycoons, mixes in easy coequal familiarity. Movie stars, high politicos, industrial magnates, authors, and scientists come and go in southeastern Arizona. No one asks for their autographs, there aren't any welcoming committees, not a telephone book is torn as they pass, and no bunting flies. In short, nobody seems to care.

I believe the reason for these anomalous social and economic

. . . and doctoring.

patterns is that the region hasn't quite outgrown the pioneer stage of development. In pioneer country, unlike the city, Man's battle for livelihood is primarily with the land. His necessitites and comforts come from his own efforts rather than through community organization. Thus, the pioneer's problems are individual, immediate, and must usually be solved by himself alone. The job at hand is all-important to a continuation of three square meals a day. So long-range, cooperative enterprises become secondary and tend to be leisure-time, cultural activites.

Where sun and wind, droughts, floods, pests, heat and cold are an active, vital part of daily living, people's surroundings are infinitely more important to them than they are to urban dwellers. Nature sits on each man's doorstep and can't be ignored, for she is boss. So natural phenomena become the chief subjects of thought and discussion, with the weather easily leading the list of absorbing topics of conversation. Even gossip takes second place.

For several years Phyllis and I raised white-faced Herefords on the Flying H. We also exhibited various livestock at fairs and took a blue ribbon for a prize 900-pound Berkshire hog. Outwardly we appeared to be established ranchers. But deep down inside we knew we were rank amateurs, not temperamentally suited to the strenuous sunrise-to-sundown schedule. Besides, the exact-

We were proud of our Beltsville white turkeys.

ing life interfered with a long-standing ambition of ours—that was to write. We'd collaborated on eight stage plays, all produced, and had interested a New York agent in handling them. True, the nearest we had come to Broadway was a little threatre on Brooklyn's Flatbush Avenue, but once the writing spark is kindled, it doesn't extinguish easily.

So Phyllis and I cast about and found a buyer for the Flying H. He was a gentleman from Minnesota who wanted to transfer his mink farm to Arizona, if he could find the right climate. He also liked the idea of cattle on the side. They could work for him while the mink slept. The ranch stretched from the San Pedro River valley to the top of the Huachuca Mountains, and its altitude ranged between five thousand feet and ninety-four hundred feet. I maintained a cooperative government weather station near the barn and showed the Minnesotan official figures proving that our summers were cooler than where he lived, with much milder winters. He was satisfied and we signed the papers. But the negotiations took a couple of months before the sale became final. During the interim Chuck Perlee visited us.

Our Herefords ranged from the foothills to the mountaintops.

Nature quickly whittles man down to size.

Chuck is Charles D. Perlee, Lively Arts Editor of the *San Bernardino Sun*. He also writes a column for the paper with his wife, Virginia. An Arizona enthusiast, Chuck came over from California for a week or two each summer as a voluntary ranch hand, to relax in the wide open spaces with crowbar, shovel, or pitchfork, and to breathe the untainted air. He and I always ended his annual visit with a few days' camping trip. This time we traversed the lofty Crest Trail in the Chiricahua Mountains, seventy miles to the northeast. On our return we took the long way around via Cave Creek Canyon and Portal. The route was new to me and brought us by the Painted Canyon Ranch for the first time. Chuck in his column told it this way:

THE PAINTED CANYON RANCH WE "BOUGHT"

One day in August Weldon Heald and Chuck set off for a hike in southeastern Arizona's fabulous Chiricahua Mountains from the

Heald's Huachuca ranch. On the way home Weldon drove down Cave Creek Canyon, when Chuck saw a sign, "Painted Canyon Ranch," with an attractive rambling ranch house overlooking an expanse of green lawn, and a natural-looking swimming pool. All around was magnificent mountain scenery. A smaller sign read "For Sale."

Chuck slammed his foot on the floor-boards and told Weldon to stop.

"What for? It's getting late," said Weldon.

"I want to see that ranch," replied Chuck.

"But I don't want to buy any more ranches," said Weldon.

"I don't care. I just want to see it!" Chuck returned.

Chuck had suddenly gotten the idea that this was where he wanted to live for the rest of his life—if he could only find an "angel" to finance a dude ranch for him. So, after much cajoling to get Weldon inside the place, we met the lovely Manhattanish creature who owned it.

Weldon showed no interest at all in buying the ranch, but he asked questions. Three days later Chuck flew home to California and immediately began asking his more affluent friends to back the project of a guest ranch in Cave Creek Canyon. It was quite fortunate that they all turned him down, because only a week later Weldon wrote:

"Remember the ranch we saw that day in the Chiricahuas? Well, Phyllis and I are buying it, and we hope you'll come over and visit us."

So the Minnesota gentleman moved to the Flying H with his family and mink, and we transferred to the Painted Canyon Ranch. There, in a tranquil remnant of the natural world, Phyllis and I hoped to devote full time to writing. All that is left to us of the Flying H are some of our liveliest memories and a silver Flying H belt buckle that I still wear.

4 The Home Grounds

In the Southwest, more than any other place I know, the residents have a genuine, deep interest in their non-human environment. On every living room table are books, well-thumbed from much use, about birds and animals, trees and wildflowers, rocks, insects, even snakes. Rarely does a conversation go on for long without reference to the natural surroundings in which a family lives. The discussion may turn to chipmunks, a newly discovered cactus, a rare hummingbird, or a nearby bed of geodes. Such people cannot help having a feeling of being one with the natural world, which eliminates any tendency to feel cut off or isolated.

Their attitude is summed up in an answer I heard a native Arizonan give to a lady visitor. She looked from the old-timer's porch over a slice of emptiness the size of Rhode Island.

"It's beautiful," she admitted, "but why do you want to live so far away?"

He turned to her in surprise. "Far away from what?" he said.

We mountain islanders fielded a similar question. We were often asked by outlanders: "Don't you get lonely way off here in such a remote spot?" The answer was a definite no.

First of all, we were much too busy. A home sixty-five miles from the nearest repairman has its special set of problems and usually the trouble, whatever it was, required immediate emergency attention.

If we phoned long-distance to Douglas for help, two men eventually arrived in a truck, like Sicilian carabinieri who always travel the hazardous back country in pairs, and the bill included time-and-a-half for overtime and portal-to-portal charges—no pun intended. The men never brought lunches, and to show our hearts and pocketbooks were in the right place Phyllis treated them to at least one rib-filling meal while they were on the job. So, all in all, we could afford this type of expert assistance only in cases of dire necessity. This meant we had to be our own plumbers, electricians, gas engineers, pipe fitters, ditch diggers, and fence stretchers. Like it or not, we were generally do-it-yourselfers.

From our experience on the Flying H, Phyllis and I were fair ranch hands, and we divided the chores at Painted Canyon. My province was mostly the practical and mechanical, while hers included care of the rabbits, chickens, and our one milk cow. She also headed the aesthetic department and was in charge of beautification. Her first major project was painting the guest house, garage, and other natural wood outbuildings white with green trim. My wife looked very professional when she went to work with buckets of paint, brushes, and ladder. However, as the days went by, her blue jeans and pullover sweater took on a startling mosaic of green and white.

"Aren't you a bit splashy?" I once inquired timidly.

"Not at all," said Phyllis lightly. "The job's coming on swimmingly."

An hour or so later, as I was typing a final manuscript, I heard a *plop* outside, followed by a canine yelp and an anguished human "Oh-h-h!" I jumped to the window, opened it, and looked out. There was Phyllis on the ladder, green from the knees down, and below, the greenest dog I've ever seen.

"What happened?" I asked foolishly.

"Beautiful started to take off after a squirrel. She jogged the ladder and the pail of paint fell smack on top of her."

We worked on Beautiful with paint remover, then gave her a soap-and-water bath, but for several weeks we had a green-tinted dog. Fortunately, she showed no ill effects. But she was very sensitive about her off-color appearance and slunk away, tail between legs, when people laughed at her. In time, though, the place gleamed in fresh white and green. There was no further incident, and Beautiful's tarnished psyche and coat slowly returned to normal.

Although surrounded by springs and running water our commonest crisis was not to have any. The main spring wasn't high

People around Portal have a deep interest in birds . . .

. . . and animals . . .

. . . trees, wildflowers, rocks . . .

enough above the house to deliver sufficient water by gravity, and
it was augmented by an electric pressure pump. I never knew the
exact causes of the pump's frequent ills, but by spending hours
cleaning, priming, replacing parts, dismantling the pump and putting it together again I could usually restore normal water pressure.

Ranch-style plumbing is the result of haphazard growth, not
over-all planning. When a new drain pipe, tank, or outlet is needed
it is put in, but not necessarily according to standard methods or
in logical places. This makes for original and complicated systems
which require considerable detective work even to locate the clogs,
back-ups, leaks, or whatever it is that's flooding the kitchen or emp-
tying the storage tank.

Our electric wiring was in the same casual class as the plumbing.
When the R. E. A. 220-volt line came up the canyon we were ad-
vised to have the electrical set-up checked. So we called Douglas
and a pair of electricians arrived one morning by truck. They
crawled up through the hatch into the attic and were gone at least

an hour. We knew by the thumpings, bangings, and muffled conversation that the situation was grave. The two descended just in time for lunch. As they sat down to the table one of them solemnly announced, "It's a miracle you folks weren't burned out of here long ago." The other nodded affirmatively over his soup. Verdict: complete re-wiring. Cost: over six hundred dollars.

With only fifty-three acres, the Painted Canyon Ranch was not a working outfit, so we resigned from the Arizona Cattle Growers Association and its feminine auxiliary, the Cowbelles. But social life in the Chiricahuas is well-organized. Unlike the city where one may not know the people in the next apartment, Phyllis and I were acquainted with nearly everybody in the Chiricahuas and had friends scattered all over southeastern Arizona. It wasn't unusual for us to attend a dinner party in Douglas, and we conducted our Huachuca Writers class every other week in Bisbee, ninety miles away. Then there were local activities. The ladies of the Sew What Club arranged tea-and-cake parties, picnics, and get-togethers of various kinds. Each spring, too, the Douglas Branch of the Arizona Bank held its annual outdoor barbecue at the ranch. Phyllis was a member of the Portal School Board, and the dozen or so pupils varied from honor students to delinquents, as children do everywhere. Many an evening I sat in on solemn meetings to solve juvenile problems. We were also on the telephone and electric power committees and our sessions were lively and often stormy. In Portal, two people sometimes agree, but seldom three.

But it was the dropper-inners who kept us from any feeling of isolation. Phyllis and I have never lived in a place where we met so many people. While we were at Painted Canyon Ranch, callers from thirty-seven states and eight foreign countries stopped by to say hello. We didn't count all the visitors, but more than five hundred signed our guest book.

To them Phyllis and I were residents of an earthly Nirvana, peaceful and trouble-free. Most of them had shed their lowland worries and responsibilities at the foot of the mountains and arrived at our doorstep carefree and lighthearted. In their euphoria they looked upon us as fortunate lotus eaters who had found a way to beat the problems and complexities of modern life.

Not the least of our problems were those that arose when guests turned up unexpectedly. Lem and Irma Banks, both native Chiricahuans who lived on a ranch up Whitetail Creek to the north, were a great help to us, particularly when we had house guests. They didn't stay with us permanently, but would come for as long as a week or two at a time. Len was an experienced and resourceful fixer-upper and handyman who saved us many a long-distance call to Douglas, while Irma was an accomplished cook, both in quality and quantity. I'll never forget the taste of her warm, oven-fresh loaves of homemade bread or the north-of-the-border Mexican meals which were better than any I've had south of it. Irma's zesty enchiladas were served flat, one on top of another, like a stack of chili-peppery pancakes.

Len and Irma weren't always around when house guests arrived, although Phyllis tried to plan it that way. Our friends had a way of jumping the schedule. I especially remember a couple from the East Coast who showed up forty-eight hours before they were due.

"We made better time driving across the continent than we expected," they explained blithely. "We knew it wouldn't make any difference on a ranch."

This was a bit wide of the mark!

After glasses of cold milk—a bovine welcome from "Mamie" —Phyllis suggested I show the guests around the place. I was surprised, but got the message. While we were on tour, she telephoned for reinforcements. Luckily the Forest Service line was working that day, and Irma promised to come and cope with dinner. Then the thoroughly unprepared hostess of Painted Canyon checked the guest cottage. She dusted, filled the bedside carafes with water, put clean towels in the bathroom, and even cut some lilac blossoms and had them on the dresser before we returned.

We got through the day in fine style. The guests never suspected that we'd been caught off-guard. Next morning Phyllis took them with her on the hundred-and-thirty-mile shopping trip to Doug-

Just quiet, serene beauty.

las for enough supplies to last the week's visit. The fact that the rear end of the station wagon sagged with the load of solid and liquid sustenance made no impression on our Eastern friends.

The second evening, as we sat on the porch sipping our nightcaps, one of them sighed contentedly and murmured with a trace of envy, "What a life! No worries. No troubles. Not even any recorded background music. Just quiet, serene beauty and time to do anything you want. You'll never get ulcers here."

The Chiricahuas are a zoological and botanical bonanza and sooner or later much of the naturalist world beat a track to our door—not because we made better mousetraps but because of our superior mice. Each year nature enthusiasts of one sort or another prospect the mountains and canyons in ever increasing numbers, seeking their particular kind of treasure. We came to accept the rather peculiar activities of our visitors. It got so we didn't even slow down on our daily trips to the post office when we'd see

A birder photographing a nest of fledglings.

a man high on a portable aluminum ladder, photographing a nest of fledgling kingbirds in a tree branch. Nor were we startled at night by the weird sight of dancing lights in the woods. That would be a couple of entomologists with miners' headlamps on their hats turning over rocks in search of choice spiders and beetles. We weren't even surprised when an eminent biologist asked one summer evening if he might take a recording of a musical frog who lived in our pond. I was proud that it briefly bore the scientific name of *Rana healdi,* until proved to be a variation of a known species. The only other object in the world named for me is the Heald Nunatak, rising from the glacial wilderness of Antarctica. Paul Siple christened the lonely rock on his last trip to Little America, but I've never been able to locate it on any map. However, in compensation, the Hoskins had a cow named Phyllis.

Maybe I was responsible for some of this influx. I spent considerable time exploring, and have written more than a half-hundred magazine articles describing the remarkable and unique features of southeastern Arizona's mountains in general, and the Chiricahuas in particular. As a result, most callers at Painted Canvon Ranch followed their introductions with questions concerning something I had written.

"Where is this waterfall you tell about?"

"Will you lead us to Crystal Cave?"

"Where can I see a coati?"

So Phyllis and I perforce became a sort of Chiricahua natural history information center.

Our scientific and nature-loving callers were friendly, sociable people, and the aroma of coffee or the sound of clinking ice usually induced them to break their esoteric activities for short periods. So, on our veranda the talk ranged over the natural world. It might be Victor Cahalane back from an African trip, decrying the hoodlum-like antics of baboons; or the late Bert Harwell summoning a feathered congregation on the front lawn with his realistic bird calls; Sir Hubert Wilkins relating submarine adventures near the North Pole; or William Woodin III exhibiting the rapid-fire tail vibrations of a lyre snake with a live specimen. Whatever the subject, it was always interesting.

5 Birds of Various Feathers

By far the greatest number of our visitors were birders. Unrealistically called bird watchers by those who have never seen them in action, these dedicated people pursue their avocation with unmatched intensity, perseverance, and single-mindedness. Each has amassed a so-called "lifetime list" of birds seen and will travel hundreds of miles, enduring any hardship or discomfort to add a new species to the "count." They descended upon us from all parts of the country, male and female, in pairs and groups. A single birder is a rarity because unless two or more spot the quarry, there is no official score. Perhaps this double check system might well be adopted for golfers in the rough. Professional ornithologists may have profound reasons for studying the tarsus of a *Buteo regulus,* but the best explanation birders give for birding is that it's fun.

Standard equipment consists of binoculars slung around the neck, ready for instant use, and a pocket-sized reference book, usually Roger Tory Peterson's *A Field Guide to Western Birds.* Some advanced members of the fraternity came in cars loaded with various paraphernalia. These included cameras fitted with telescope lenses and stroboscopic light capable of photographically "freezing" a hummingbird's wings beating at the fantastic rate of fifty to seventy times a second. Several of the avian pictorial experts were on assignment for illustrations in the *National Geographic, Life Nature Library,* and other publications.

When good birders die they will undoubtedly go to a sky island heaven resembling the Chiricahuas. Herbert Brandt in his sumptuous and authoritative volume, *Arizona and its Birdlife,* writes: "There are a few less than 650 full species of birds now breeding north of Mexico, including Alaska, Greenland, and Lower California. I found that one-fourth, or 170, nest in an area

43

of ten thousand square miles located in the southeastern corner of Arizona, and many of these . . . are the rarer, little known kinds." In fact, the lucky birder will spot some of the continent's rarest species in the Chiricahuas and in the Huachuca and Santa Rita mountains, farther west. The Chiricahuas alone have six species of hummingbirds, sixteen of flycatchers, five of thrashers, twelve of owls, eleven of warblers, fourteen of hawks and eagles, and five of jays and ravens.

Sorting out and identifying each of these correctly is a confusing job, but our determined birders accomplished it and in the process uncovered such rarities as the spotted screech owl, zone-tailed hawk, xantus's becard, rivoli's and blue-throated hummingbirds, and the sulphur-bellied flycatcher. Others, equally localized but more often seen, are the Arizona woodpecker, Arizona jay, bridled titmouse, red-faced warbler, and the Mexican chickadee. The last inhabits such a restricted range that bird guides list it as being found only in the Chiricahua Mountains at elevations of seven to ten thousand feet, an area smaller than that of New York City.

However, the prize find is the gaudy green and red coppery-tailed trogon. This *rara avis* is a status symbol which confers distinction to any lifetime list, and seeing one is the ambition of every birder visiting southeastern Arizona. But the odds are about the same as hitting the jackpot at Las Vegas. This brilliant, par-

Birders in action.

rot-like bird is so retiring that one ornithologist and his wife stalked the remote canyons of our rugged sky island each spring for ten years before they found a trogon family nesting near a Cave Creek campground, not a hundred feet from the road.

The coppery-tailed variety is a representative of a distinct order of birds living in the tropics of America, Africa, and Asia. Of the thirty-five species it is the only trogon found in the United States, its range extending a few miles north of the Mexican border into three limited localities in the mountains of southeastern Arizona. The Chiricahuas are one of them. Trogons are noted for their dazzling contrasting colors which glow with exquisite tints of pink, crimson, orange, brown, and shiny metallic green. Most famous of the tribe is the long-tailed trogon or quetzal of Central America. Considered by many to be the most beautiful bird in the world, it was the sacred symbol of Quetzalcoatl, nature god of the Toltecs and Aztecs.

Our single species has an overall length of about a foot. The male's head and neck are a dark glossy green separated from a bright rose-red body by a white collar, and the moderately long tail is copper tinged. The female is similar, but head and upper parts are brown, while the body is a less vivid red. Their favorite nesting places are holes in trees along mountain canyons between forty-five and sixty-five hundred feet elevation. They feed on in-

sects, fruits, and small lizards. Although visually resplendent, these exotic birds have miserable voices; their call resembles the rapid series of low, hoarse notes of a hen turkey. Undoubtedly, a few families of coppery-tailed trogons nest in the Chiricahuas each spring. But they are so chary of civilization that several years may pass without their secluded havens being discovered. It was our job as wildlife information center to know when one had been found, for almost always the first question asked by ardent birders was: "Where can we see a trogon?"

Formerly an even rarer southern bird occasionally crossed the border and tarried briefly in the Chiricahuas, although it never nested there. This was the heavily-built, green, thick-billed parrot. Often up to sixteen inches long, it must have been a sight to behold, with coal-black bill and orange forehead. Old-timers tell that at intervals of several years hundreds of these tropical nomads flocked through the woods for a few days, then completely vanished. The species is listed in bird guides as the only surviving parrot in the country, but that may be hopeful optimism, as the last recorded visitation occurred more than thirty years ago.

Nonetheless, the Chiricahuas and thick-billed parrots still have a sentimental bond. The San Diego Zoo acquired a pair in 1956. The hope was that they would breed. But nine childless years went by.

"It was beginning to look fruitless," said K. C. Lint, curator of birds. "We thought we had matched their natural diet morsel for morsel.

"But we had missed the nuts from pinyon pine cones. So we had them collected and shipped to us from the Chiricahua Mountains. Apparently that turned the trick."

At any rate, the first thick-billed parrot ever born in captivity arrived on September 13, 1965.

"The native Eastern parrots and parakeets are gone and man's invasion of the wilds has dangerously thinned out the thick bills," says Mr. Lint. "We'd hate to see another species go, especially one this beautiful."

Although the Chiricahuas are not on any well-established north-south flyway, the number and variety of birds, both migrants and strays, is surprising. One morning, while we were taking a coffee break on the veranda, a whir of many wings drew our attention to a band of at least fifty birds unknown to us. They gracefully swung and turned in perfect formation as they circled the meadow, first flashing white, then black in the bright sunlight. We watched them, fascinated, until they departed as suddenly as they had come.

"The book! The book!" we both shouted.

The picture and description exactly fitted the swallow-tailed kite, even to its distinctive elongated forked tail. This bird of the Deep South has no business in Arizona. It has never been observed west of the Rio Grande, so far as I know, and this one sight record is so unusual that some people raise a polite but incredulous eyebrow.

Our abundance of water in a generally arid land was a particular attraction to birds. We saw wood ibis at Herb Martyr Dam above us on Cave Creek, and once a great blue heron, while one dry fall day a host of mallard ducks splashed down in our pool on their way south and paddled around briefly. Again, an unfamiliar grating call announced the arrival of a pair of western belted kingfishers. For several hours they flitted from branch to branch among the big trees around the house, then left. We welcomed them as newcomers to our list, but next day found that they had grossly abused our hospitality. The nine lusty goldfish were gone from the pond and with them the third generation of babies to be reared there. Our enthusiasm for birds suffered a definite setback.

Seasonal migrations at Painted Canyon Ranch are vertical as well as horizontal. Many birds that summer on the mountaintops descend to the canyons in winter. Among them are the spritely, yellow-eyed Arizona juncos, dwellers of the upper forests, who gathered in busily pecking groups on our front lawn during the cold weather. The wild turkeys, too, made their winter home with us. At night they perched high in the sycamores, their big black shapes making an eerie sight when the moon shone.

Phyllis and I never put out food for the birds nor tried to tempt them with artificial lures. They were a part of our natural surroundings and we liked it that way. Our feathered visitors had to take things as they were—including the cats. And they did. Cats vary, just as people do, and it's been our experience that if they are well fed regularly since kittenhood, they show little interest in birds. So far as we know, Barney, Pinky, and Whitey never caught a bird or even crouched ready to spring, with twitching tails and waggling behinds. On the other hand, we learned that most birds can take care of themselves, and some made our cats' lives miserable during nesting time.

In other words, to us, birds were just one of the many ingredients which made life in the Chiricahuas a zestful adventure. Neither of us became birders, and we shamefully admitted when questioned that we had no lifetime lists. But our deep feeling is that it isn't necessary to know the names, pedigrees, and chemical composition of objects in order to enjoy them. This is an age of specialists, but most of them I know miss a lot. We met birders whose eyes saw only feathers; rockhounds who missed the view because what they sought was at their feet; photographers who believed the only good color shots were flowers; and fishermen whose interests were wholly sub-aqueous.

Better, it seems to me, is to be a general practitioner of the out-of-doors, and let who will be specialists. Knowing a little about a great deal can be more satisfying than knowing a great deal about a very little. In that way one gains an awareness of the multiple wonders of this amazing sky island and becomes rich in experience and fulfillment.

6 Fur, and More Feathers

When things go wrong around Portal, as they often do, old-timers shake their heads and mutter, "It's the Curse of Geronimo!" The story goes that when the Apache's last chief was captured, he raised fists high above his head and called down a curse upon the country and the white men who had stolen it from his people. I'm not superstitious, but perhaps there is more to this than mere legend. For, sometimes it seems as if the malevolence of the ruthless Indian leader still haunts the Chiricahua's rugged canyons and ridges.

If so, I think I discovered the reason.

On my first hike up the Silver Peak trail, I stopped near the top to rest. Turning, I gave an involuntary start. There, outlined against the blue Southwestern sky, was a gigantic profile of an Indian, stolidly gazing out over the hills, valleys, grasslands and deserts, three thousand feet below.

"It's Geronimo!" I exclaimed aloud.

Nobody had mentioned this great stone face, and it is apparently unknown to the local inhabitants. Yet it is in plain view from the trail and so perfect in all details that it would be celebrated in a more populated region.

Here, on the edge of a cliff, Nature has carved through the centuries a profile four times larger than the man-made faces at South Dakota's Mount Rushmore Memorial. Rising at least two hundred and fifty feet from chin to top of head, it is complete with nothing skimped, caricatured, or left to the imagination. There is a mouth, an eye, and a great jutting nose, while the wrinkles around the mouth, cheek, and eye are surprisingly realistic. In outline the face resembles that of a brooding Indian, the likeness being doubly strong because the rock is a warm, red-brown latite lava, almost the exact color of an Indian's skin.

I stood fascinated. The silence was complete and the ageless

49

stone profile cast an eerie spell over the place. The sense of time and space was gone and I felt a powerful and immediate awareness of the stalwart race of red men who once roamed these wild mountains. The feeling was one of awe closely akin to fear. I don't know how long the mood lasted; it was suddenly broken by a scolding chipmunk in a nearby tree. But as I plodded up the trail once more the thought struck me that maybe the Curse of Geronimo wasn't a myth after all. Perhaps the Great Spirit of the Apaches had turned the chief to stone and set his face high in the Chiricahuas to look over the lost homeland of his people and harass the white intruders through eternity.

I wouldn't want to vouch for this—but it could be.

Whether or not it was simply the Curse of Geronimo, we began to lose chickens. Each morning at roll call the flock would be missing one or two members. When our prize rooster disappeared, we felt vigorous action was indicated. So Len Banks constructed a box trap and baited it with meat scraps. He set the aromatic snare beside the chicken yard and a couple of mornings later brought it back with the perpetrator of the "fowl" deed inside. It was a ringtail cat. Of course Phyllis adopted the little animal, and as "Ringo" he soon became a household pet along with Beautiful and the cats. In fact, we all got along fine together. But Ringo vanished after a three-months' stay and we never saw him again. Nevertheless, his friendliness and good manners won him a warm place in our hearts.

The ringtail cat's principal home is Mexico, but it roams as far north as southeastern Oregon and parts of Utah and Colorado. Known as civet cat, bassarisk, mountain cat, hydrophobia skunk, and *cacomistl* in Mexico, the ringtail is neither cat nor skunk, but a relative of the raccoons, which it somewhat resembles. Full-grown adults measure fourteen to sixteen inches long and weigh about two and a half pounds. By far the most striking feature of the ringtail cat is the handsome bushy tail, often a foot and a half in length, which is banded with alternating black and white stripes. The ringtail's face is more pointed than a raccoon's, giving him an intense inquiring look, and the color of his silky hair varies from buff on the back to white below.

The profile of an Indian stolidly gazing out over hills and valleys.

This engaging little creature is intelligent, retiring, and helpful to Man in keeping down rats and mice. But he has an undeservedly bad reputation, perhaps because of a fondness for chicken. Recently a big-circulation outdoors magazine carried an article on the ringtail cat, calling him a savage killer and the fiercest fighter for his weight in the animal kingdom. It suggested that even humans aren't safe from unprovoked attack. Such exaggerations are often used by the gun fraternity as psychological justification for killing small, inoffensive, non-edible animals. It is dignified by the name of predator control, and gives hunters the ennobling illusion that they are doing a valuable public service by ridding the world of ravening wild beasts. I don't know what ringtails the author of the article was acquainted with, but he certainly didn't know Ringo. A more gentle, good-natured guest we never had at the ranch.

He liked best a cross-ceiling beam in the dining room, that had space on top for a snug retreat. Ringtails have semi-retractable claws, and this high perch probably reminded him of his home in the trees or on some steep rocky cliff. We'd leave food on the buffet and watch him clamber down the wooden upright, looking cautiously from side to side. It didn't matter much what we put out for him. He would eat it hungrily, and then scramble back to his hideout. Ringo's large ears, directed forward to catch the slightest hostile sound, were in constant motion, while his tail swished back and forth and his whiskers twitched continuously. Most appealing were his big, soft, expressive eyes—the brightest I've ever seen in an animal.

This was the only wild ringtail we met in the Chiricahuas, although I ran across their round cat-like footprints in the snow. For they live in fairly inaccessible places and only forage at night. One morning a couple of months after Ringo disappeared, two more chickens were missing. Phyllis and I wondered if the culprits were Ringo and his pals. We could almost imagine him saying in ringtail language, "Come on boys, I know where we can get some plump ones!" I don't condone stealing, but we often served chicken to our human guests and felt that this was the least we could do to reward a very likeable visitor for helping the cats keep the place free of varmints of all kinds. But whether it was Ringo or not, that was the last of the chicken stealing.

"Gorgeous" and "Lovely" weren't really guests, but rather members of the family. However, after the latter's shocking defection, we were tempted to disown her, and seldom referred afterwards to her scandalous behavior. Gorgeous was a proud East Indian peacock and Lovely was his mate. For many months theirs was a happy connubial life. They ambled sedately about the grounds by day and roosted high in a sycamore at night. Each morning the pair thumped down on the roof of the house, and Gorgeous greeted the rising sun from the ridgepole with loud foghorn honks. He was our alarm clock. If the day were frigid both

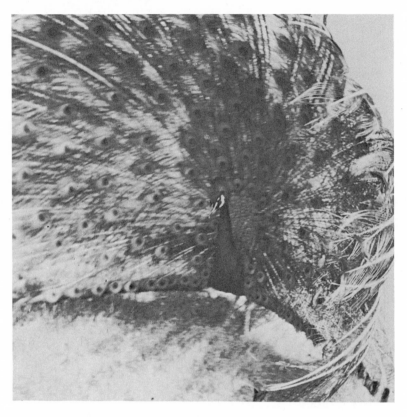

"Shake 'em up!"

huddled atop the chimney, warmed by the ascending heat from the fireplace. Almost always they formed a part of the familiar domestic scene in one direction or another.

Gorgeous was arrayed in feathered vestments of blue and shimmering metallic green, befitting his status as monarch of birds, and his tail swept the ground with the regality of a king's coronation robes. He knew he was a very grand sight and, like most peacocks, was an inveterate exhibitionist. When I said to him, "Shake 'em up. Shake 'em up," he majestically raised his six-foot semi-circle of tail coverts and paced regally back and forth in front of me. Now and then he stopped and posed in different positions like a professional model, feathers aquiver with a soft rustling sound.

We hung a large mirror on the fence at the edge of the lawn.

Gorgeous spent many hours preening before it, either admiring his reflection or showing off for what he believed to be another bird. When Dr. Percival Symonds, Columbia psychology professor, visited Painted Canyon he became so interested in this moot question that he asked us to study our peacock's reactions and give an opinion. After closely observing the mirror act for some time, Phyllis and I decided Gorgeous well knew whom he was admiring.

But these masculine blandishments weren't sufficient to hold the flighty female of the species. One afternoon Lovely eloped with a flock of wild turkeys. In her defense I must admit there is something symbolically virile and compelling about an untamed tom. He is the caveman of the bird world. The peacock struts; the turkey swaggers. Poor Gorgeous was never the same afterwards. His ego deflated like a pricked balloon. For several days he searched for his missing mate, stopping now and again to call loudly and listen for an answer. When this failed he sought solace in human companionship, sitting morose and immovable beside us on the veranda. My "Shake 'em up. Shake 'em up!" brought no response. He took to invading the house, and we'd find him perched on the living room table or on my bed, his exquisite tail feathers spread across the covers. We kept up hope as the days went by that Lovely would come to her senses, if she had any, and return to her true love. But she never did. For some time people reported seeing her with the flock of turkeys in the high meadows near Rustler Park. Her eventual fate is wrapped in mystery.

We had seen evidence of this apparent affinity between peafowl and turkeys before. Both birds belong to the pheasant family and have many similar characteristics and habits, as well as anatomic parallels. But they are by no means closely related. On the Flying H Ranch Phyllis and I had two white peacocks named "Carrara" and "Alabaster," who wandered freely over the premises. We also raised small Beltsville White turkeys for the market. They were enclosed in pens behind six-foot wire fences, but the barrier was no obstacle to our amorous peacocks. Several times they sailed over the top and landed square in the midst of the fluttering turkey hens.

The toms, resenting the violation of their harems, would rush the peacocks and promptly knock them out cold. Once we thought Alabaster had been killed after such an encounter. Phyllis and I found him in a turkey pen motionless on his back, his feet sticking straight up and his tail in the dust, some of the feathers twisted and broken. Over him stood a big tom still chortling a victory chant. We dragged the defeated bird outside the fence and tossed a pail full of water on him. He came to life, jumped up, shook hard, and honked like a French taxi as he strode off. This should have taught the peacocks a lesson, but it didn't. Several days later both Carrara and Alabaster again visited the turkey hens with the same dire results.

"Time assuages sorrow" even in the peacock world, and after a couple of weeks Gorgeous once more assumed the role of king of the Painted Canyon Ranch, but without his docile consort.

Our experience with Muscovy ducks was fortunately brief. The Kents, who operate the Silver Spur Guest Ranch on the west side of the mountains, presented us with a pair of the big, fat, overgrown waddlers, and we installed them down by the pool. That was a mistake. From then on they took complete possession and

There is something compelling about an untamed tom.

resented any intrusion into their private preserve. Whenever we went to the pool for a dip, the pair of Muscovies rushed at us with venomous hisses and wide-open bills. Beautiful fared even worse. Once we heard a yipping and saw her racing from the vicinity of the pool with a twelve-pound duck hanging from her tail. The Muscovies were an example of what sheer audacity and presumption can do. They were the most belligerent and ill-tempered of any creatures we've ever met, yet they were almost as defenseless as rabbits. We put up with them for awhile. Then Len and Irma kindly took them off our hands, and neither Phyllis nor I inquired what became of them.

7 *Wildlife Panorama*

Although birds were the most lively and vociferous visitors at Painted Canyon Ranch, hardly a day passed without encounters with our shier animal neighbors. The natural world pressed close on all sides and was the predominating influence around us. There the cycle of life went on much as it has for thousands of years. The sun shone and the rain fell, plants flourished and died to enrich the soil, insects thrived on the vegetation, other creatures drew life from the insects, and so on up through amphibians, reptiles, birds and mammals to the largest carnivores. Each had a special niche and was at home in its particular environment. And all were intricately interconnected in an endless chain of mutual help and destruction in which each link was an integral part of the whole. Man, the all-consuming animal, had not completely disturbed the natural order of things.

Phyllis and I realized we were temporary intruders. We occupied an advance outpost in beleaguered territory. Human civilization was not far behind and advancing rapidly. Already its disrupting force had altered the primeval realm of the Chiricahuas. The mighty grizzly was gone; except for wanderers from south of the border, the wolf has disappeared; bighorn sheep no longer stand guard atop the highest peaks and ridges; and domestic cattle compete with the wild inhabitants for grass and forage. Nevertheless, our surroundings were still a huge near-natural zoo, aviary, and botanical garden—of its kind perhaps unrivaled on the continent—and both of us marvelled at its infinite diversity and delicately adjusted complexity. At Painted Canyon Ranch we were constantly impressed with the grandeur and importance of the non-human world.

Of all the wildlife, we became most familiar with the deer.

Everywhere Rocky Mountain mule deer and whitetail deer roam the Chiricahuas from the wooded canyons to the summit forests. Almost every day one, two, or a half-dozen bucks and does could be seen peacefully browsing our meadows. Sometimes the young accompanied their elders; one time we found a new-born fawn alone in a comfortable bed of pine needles not a quarter mile from the house.

Beautiful delighted in an occasional night chase with the deer, apparently driven by some atavistic urge inherited from her Scottish Highland ancestors. Now and then we were awakened by sharp, short barks as she pursued her fleet quarry through the woods across the creek. She was hopelessly outclassed, of course, as a leaping and bounding whitetail can travel at a top speed of thirty-five miles an hour. Presumably these nocturnal frolics were enjoyed on both sides, as the deer would be back next day ready for another go whenever Beautiful gave the starting signal.

Living with deer had its drawbacks. They were so plentiful that we were forced to become experts at split-second braking when they made sudden, startled bolts across the road directly in front of the car. Then, deer not only raided our vegetable garden as if it were a big salad bowl, but they developed a taste for our apples. In abysmal ignorance we repaired the five-foot fence enclosing the orchard, but soon found we should have made it at least three feet higher to be an effective barrier against the whitetails' prodigious high jumps. True, our Baldwins weren't the pampered, full-blown favorites of commerce. We let them fend pretty much for themselves. But what they lacked in size and juiciness, they made up in the tart, winy flavor of wild apples which have had to put up a fight for existence. Anyway, there was a market of sorts for them, and we estimated that playing hosts to deer cost us a couple of hundred dollars annually.

Once a year the deer completely deserted us. That was during the fall hunting season. At the onset of this hazardous period some kind of cervine telepathy warned them to strike out for the remotest canyons and roughest slopes. Even there they weren't safe. For two weeks the mountains were invaded by a host of determined sportsmen clad in red jackets and caps and armed with high-powered, long-range rifles. Gun shots echoed near and far, camp-grounds were crowded, and a parade of cars passed by, their hoods draped with limp and lifeless trophies. We tied a ribbon with a big red bow around Beautiful's neck and all of us prudently stayed close to home until quiet reigned once more and the survivors of the hunt cautiously returned to browse the meadows and munch our apples.

In spite of the annual onslaught, there are about fifteen hundred deer of both kinds in the Chiricahuas, and the concentration of whitetails is the heaviest in the Southwest. This is the result of planned game management and its sole purpose is, by artificial stimulus, to provide hunters with an abundant supply of their favorite moving targets. It is achieved by stringent game laws, rigidly enforced, and the ruthless elimination of so-called predators. The two-weeks open season is a part of the program to prevent the situation from getting out of hand, and is referred to in game-management parlance as a "harvest of the increment."

This system tends to produce an overpopulation of deer which puts a strain on the available food supply, denudes vegetation, and causes damaging erosion. In fact, we Chiricahuans who lived under the strict edicts of the Arizona Game and Fish Department sometimes felt our position was similar to peasants of old in a royal hunting park, surrounded by privileged stags reserved for the king's exclusive use.

Because of its predilection for venison on the hoof and other antisocial characteristics, the mountain lion heads the list of the Chiricahuas' Most Wanted Predators. Although animal organisms have preyed upon each other since life emerged from the Cambrian ooze, a predator today in this Man-crowded world is a nefarious Public Enemy. Broadly defined, it is any creature that destroys another which humans kill for food or for pleasure. The mountain lion is guilty on both counts. Indicted, judged, and condemned, the penalty is the firing squad.

Weighing up to two hundred pounds, and seven feet long from nose to tip of tail, this alert and agile bundle of muscle is a close relative of the African lions and tigers. Next to the jaguar, it is the largest and most formidable member of the widespread

American cat family from Argentina to Canada. With a lethal, lightning spring and unequalled feline intelligence and cunning, the mountain lion is sudden death to nearly every other wild animal in its path and often dines on calves, colts, sheep, pigs, dogs, and chickens. Man alone the big cats avoid openly, and there are few authentic cases of unprovoked attacks on humans. Even to see a mountain lion is a rare and notable experience. So far as I know none paid us stealthy night visits at Painted Canyon Ranch, and we never heard the mountain lion's legendary blood-curdling scream "like a tortured woman."

These furtive and crafty animals known also as cougars, panthers, pumas, painters, and catamounts, formerly roamed the continent's forests, mountains, plains, and deserts from coast to coast. They are adept at hit-and-run guerrilla tactics, and their raids and depredations have harassed mankind for three centuries. In retaliation a grim war of extermination has been waged against them with no quarter given. As a result the big cats have been eradicated from the eastern part of their range and are now making last-ditch stands in the wilder and more remote mountainous sections of the Far West.

The Chiricahuas are one of these lion strongholds. There a hard-pressed remnant of this once extensive and powerful race seems to be holding its own. One year seven were killed in Cave Creek basin above us, and old-timers say that there are as many today as fifty years ago. Informed guesses put the Chiricahua lion population at about thirty strays, visitors, and residents. A steady back-door influx of newcomers from Mexico is supposed to keep the supply replenished.

Professional lion hunters conduct parties into the mountains, furnishing guides, horses, camping equipment, a brace of trained hounds, and usually a guarantee of success. However, tracking down mountain lions is not for those of faint heart or faltering spirit. It means hours, sometimes days, of cold-trailing over incredibly rough country, across rock slides, through brush, and along precipitous ridges. Eventually the dogs pick up a fresh scent, and with yelps of excitement, they are off.

Following a jumped lion wherever he may lead is the thrilling

Cave Creek Canyon, incredibly rough country.

climax of the hunt. Rugged sportsmen with cougar in their blood wax lyrical about the music of the wildly clamoring hounds, the straining horses, and the tingling feeling of suspense. The denouement comes with a treed lion crouched on a limb, spitting and snarling in fury at the leaping dogs below. Even now he may spring a full thirty feet and escape to another tree, but sooner or later well-aimed shots do him in. The business is over—a successful hunt accomplished, another pernicious predator gone, a public service performed, and a state-paid bounty of seventy-five dollars to collect.

A persistent campaign of vilification and character assassination has given the mountain lion an exaggerated reputation for cruelty and wanton destruction. However, in many years of wandering the eleven "Lower Forty-eight" Far Western states I have never found evidence of his supposed frightful carnage among deer and other wildlife. Nor during the time we raised cattle and horses in southern Arizona were any of our calves or colts taken by mountain lions. Biologists and ecologists have clearly shown that these native American predators serve as natural balance wheels in the wildlife community. This is becoming increasingly apparent, and recently bounties have been wisely repealed in California, Oregon, Washington, and British Columbia. The mountain lion is a part of our rapidly vanishing wilderness heritage and should be given asylum in the few sections of primitive America we are striving to preserve intact and inviolate for the enjoyment, education, and inspiration of generations to come. Unnatural hordes of tame, liquid-eyed, semi-domestic deer are a poor substitute for our magnificent and varied original wildlife.

The ocelot is another member of the cat tribe who now and again strays north of the Mexican border. About the size of a wildcat, this nocturnal animal is handsomely marked with irregular stripes, bands, and dots on a tan background, no two individual designs being quite the same. But ocelots may have finally abandoned southern Arizona's sky islands, for not one has been reported in several years.

At night our headlights sometimes picked out the cougar's smaller cousin, the bobcat, slinking across the road in front of us, and once we slowed to allow a mother and two kittens to pass. Foxes we saw aplenty, but never got well acquainted with them in spite of their curiosity. Occasionally they sat bolt upright, watching our activities around the ranch with absorbed interest, but always at a distance. Porcupines, too, visited us, and we found they could be coaxed to the kitchen door with lettuce. There they would sit back on their fat haunches and nibble the long leaves which slowly disappeared inch by inch like green ticker tape. In fact most of our wild neighbors responded to our live-and-let-live policy and gradually became accustomed to us. I believe they actually felt that there were definite advantages to be gained in making our acquaintance.

Quite at home among desert cactus or mountain pine and fir are the peccaries, distant relatives of the Old World wild boars. Locally called javelinas, with the "j" pronounced as "h", they are tough, chunky, pig-like animals weighing up to fifty pounds, with stiff, bristly, black and grayish hair, and protruding needle-sharp tusks. Peccaries often travel in large droves, and I have seen as many as twenty trooping across the rocky desert foothills of the Santa Catalina Mountains near Tucson. Although the white-lipped species of central Mexico is larger and more aggressive, the collared peccary of Arizona is considered dangerous when cornered, because of its fearsome-looking tusks. Hair-raising tales are told of hordes of these supposedly fierce wild pigs running people up trees and keeping them prisoners there, but there is some difference of opinion about the degree of their hostility. I have never heard of the collared species attacking a man. However, they show no fear whatever and every javelina I have met was as good as I am —knew it, and knew that I knew it. My experience with them in the Chiricahuas was limited to single individuals, but that was sufficient. Once I passed within twenty feet of a large male on the Snowshed Trail above the ranch. Instead of retreating, he stood without moving a muscle, watching me suspiciously with his little beady black eyes until I disappeared around a bend. Any uneasiness there was during the encounter certainly wasn't the peccary's.

Then there is the coati or coatimundi, a surprising "believe it or not" tropical animal of Central America and Mexico that in recent years has extended its range into southern Arizona's mountains. Nobody knows why. Pronounced the Spanish way, *co-ah'-ti*, it is a member of the same family as the raccoon, which it vaguely resembles in a burlesque sort of way. If biologically possible, the crossing of a raccoon with a monkey, cat, and anteater might produce something that looks like a coati.

It has a long body covered with grayish or brown fur and a longer banded tail, often more than two feet in length. Forward it is streamlined into an elongated, pointed, upturned snout. Coatis are expert tree climbers and hold their tails in an upright position, using them much as a tightrope walker does a balance pole. They feed on berries, lizards, insects, birds' eggs, and sometimes small birds. Locally called chulas, these queer, hodgepodge animals are supposed to be ferocious and bloodthirsty. Although their tails are not prehensile, legend has it that coatis hang by them from branches and drop down to eviscerate with their cat-like claws innocent, unsuspecting dogs that just by chance happen to be passing by. It's true a chula will defend itself against an attacking dog—and who can blame it?—but in general they are harmless, good-natured animals which can easily be made desirable pets.

One family of coatis, mother, father, and a couple of youngsters, lived for a season at the end of the road up the South Fork of Cave Creek and kept the campgrounds well-policed. On several occasions I watched them carry away everything eatable the campers had left. But the largest concentration of Arizona chulas is in the Huachuca Mountains in the pine woods high up on the Reef. One time I encountered them crossing the Reef Road. I stopped the jeep and waited fully three minutes while dozens of coatis—big ones, medium-sized, and troops of babies little bigger than kittens—scurried by. On another visit at least fifty coatis dropped from tree branches and slithered down pine trunks all around me. They made off through the woods with a sound in the dead leaves and needles like a heavy downpour of rain. In neither case did the animals appear particularly frightened.

So all around us were furred and feathered neighbors, but as Nature is niggardly with water in southern Arizona, the finny

Upper Cave Creek.

tribes were sparsely represented. Several streams are perennial
but at low water even these have bone-dry stretches. Our rainbow
trout in the creek beyond the meadow were not unique; in my
wanderings I did discover a half dozen year-round pools in the
high country that contained a few trout. But we didn't reveal their
whereabouts in our Nature Information Service.

However, two dams have been built in the mountains forming
artificial ponds that are regularly stocked. These are popular with
local fishermen. Herb Martyr Dam on Cave Creek, at the end of a
side road two miles above the ranch, creates a pint-sized fishing
hole which is the source of most of the trout dinners around

This is living!

Portal. Two or three times each season the huge tank truck of the Game and Fish Department lumbered by with supplies of legal-size rainbows for Herb Martyr. Behind it came a line of cars filled with expectant anglers. No sooner was a plant made than the shores of the pond bristled with rods and the majority of trout were pulled out before they had a chance to inspect their new home. The procedure would have been simpler and more efficient if everybody brought a pail and the fish were doled out directly from the tank truck.

But Herb Martyr always harbored a few wary and sophisticated rainbows who escaped the concerted offensives, and no one was more skillful than Bill Hoskins in luring them from their hiding places. His generosity provided us with several fish fries each summer. We cooked the trout outdoors on hot flat rocks to a sizzling, aromatic, golden brown and, holding head and tail in our fingers, nibbled them like corn on the cob.

An often quoted statement of Thoreau's is: "In wildness is the preservation of the world." I'm not sure I quite understood its meaning until we lived in the heart of the Chiricahua Mountains. The venture was an escape certainly, a partial release from the increasing strains and pressures of our atomic, computerized, space-age civilization. But I believe it was an escape to reality rather than away from it. By insulating himself from the rest of Nature, Man has lost contact with his origins and background and is being jet-propelled into an uncertain future at an ever-accelerating rate.

I think most of our callers sensed the reality of the natural world as still the basic foundation of the human race. Almost invariably they settled down on our veranda, looked up at the glowing cliffs of Cave Creek Canyon to the vault of blue sky above, breathed deeply, and exclaimed:

"Ah, this is living!"

8 *Focus On Bears*

Of all the Chiricahua's wild inhabitants, bears were my favorites. But this sentimental fondness was purely theoretical, and I voluntarily kept close contacts with them to a minimum. In this, I followed the sage advice of a Sequoia National Park ranger who tells tourists: "The best way to approach a bear is, don't." I'm somewhat like the man who followed one in the snow all afternoon, but quit along about sundown because the tracks were getting "too darn fresh."

A couple of dozen black bears live in the heavy evergreen forests and open meadows along the summit of the range. "Black bear" is the name of the species, but not necessarily the color, because individuals vary from glossy anthracite, through brown to reddish cinnamon, often in the same litter. They are retiring and seldom seen; for two years I never caught sight of one. But everywhere along the high trails were signs that bears are active members of the wilderness community. Like humans, they are omnivorous and will eat anything, big or little, that walks, flies, crawls or hops, as well as anything that grows. So in the upper forests one runs across ursine excavations for ants and grubs, peeled bark indicating forays for beetles, claw-sharpening furrows in logs, and trail markers torn down, broken in two, and thoroughly chewed around the edges.

Only occasionally could I inveigle Phyllis into the high country. Although she's an outdoor girl to a point, the brand of outdoors available at Painted Canyon Ranch usually satisfied her. However, one pleasant summer afternoon I coaxed her to the road-end at Rustler Park for a leisurely climb of Flys Peak. After an hour's stroll through the sun-dappled forest we stopped at a breezy ledge on the crest to enjoy the tremendous view westward over Sulphur Spring Valley to the distant blue mountains rimming the horizon.

For a few minutes we let peace, quiet, and sunshine soak into us. Then the mountaintop tranquility was rudely broken by a loud scratching behind us. We looked around and saw what I first thought was a porcupine high in a dead spruce. But it wasn't. It was a bear's head peering at us around the trunk. Bruin had a startled look, and I expect we did too. The tableau held for a few seconds. Then the bear decided to leave. He slid down the tree with the speed of a fireman on a brass pole, chunks of dead bark flying in all directions. At the bottom he took to the woods and lumbered off at top speed, grunting like an enormous pig. He was a big fellow with a jet-black coat, weighing maybe 350 pounds. As we plodded along upwards we were just as pleased he had voted to leave this part of the mountain to us.

"First time I've seen a bear up here," I said brightly. "It probably won't happen again."

Phyllis didn't say anything.

I was wrong. We hadn't gone a quarter-mile when we were brought up short by a sound resembling a baby crying. Cautiously moving forward, we soon spotted a little bear cub far up in a spiry white fir. He was wailing piteously in a voice so human it was startling. Below stood Mama Bear looking up and giving encouraging maternal growls. Neither of them saw us, but apparently Papa had come this way and warned them that dread humans were in the offing and to get going. Having heard at my mother's knee and elsewhere that it is wisest to let mama bears and their young transact the business of living undisturbed, we stayed perfectly quiet. Little by little the cub made his perilous descent, crying all the while, until, finally reaching the ground, he hastily followed Mama into the heavy spruce thickets. Phyllis and I made a wide detour around the center of activity, and the rest of the trip was bearless.

Along the Crest Trail no place is pleasanter than Junction Saddle. Located at an altitude of 9,500 feet, just north of Chiricahua Peak, it is a gentle green swale in the forest with parklike conifers spaced far enough apart to let in a flood of subdued golden light. The air is redolent of pine needles and aromatic growing things; the sounds are the muted soughing of the wind in the treetops and the chattering of long-crested jays among the branches. I always stopped at Junction Saddle and sat with my back against a log for a

Black bear.

contemplative smoke. Meditation is far too pompous a word to use for these reveries, as it connotes mental activity, even intellectuality. I simply indulged in a passive receptivity and let the wilderness pour its strength into me. The usual assertive individual ego was exorcized, and I seemed to become a part of the universal life force. I don't wish here to appear to be emulating California's famed writer-naturalist, John Muir. He was not of my generation nor temperamental makeup. But at these times I understood his passion for the wilderness and his regret at the tragedy of its passing.

One crisp October morning I dropped into Junction Saddle, looking forward to my usual therapeutic interlude, to find I was not alone. Some fifty feet from my special log was a bear. I stopped and my heart stopped at the same time, as it was one of the biggest bears I ever met.

Serenely unaware of me, he stood upright on his hind legs against a large pine and was busily engaged in pulling at a trail sign with upstretched front claws. He made a stunning picture with the sun shining on his thick cinnamon fur. I coughed politely. The bear looked in my direction, but didn't see me and returned his attention to the sign. However, the sound must have bothered him, because in a few seconds he dropped to the ground and started up the trail toward me to investigate.

I love Nature, but not this much. So I shuffled my feet in the dry leaves. The bear stopped, gave me a surprised look, then turned and broke into a clumsy gallop, emitting hoarse grunts as he ran. Suddenly, two smaller bears that I hadn't seen before started shinnying up tree trunks. But the guttural warnings of the big bear must have said, "Follow me," for they dropped to the ground as he raced by and tailed him over the ridge. In thirty seconds not a sound broke the stillness of Junction Saddle—except for the throbbing in my ears which took some time to quiet down.

Some authorities state that all black bears hibernate in winter, usually from November to April. But there's doubt that southern Arizona bears do so. They probably sleep off and on during the cold season, but move about between naps, as I've seen bear tracks every month of the year. On the other hand, I have never run across any snug winter dens such as northern bears prepare for themselves; Chiricahua bruins seem satisfied to hole up for short periods any place that offers a fair promise of privacy and protection.

Unfortunately, fall and winter is a time when the more adventurous of the bear clan are apt to descend into the canyons to see if the pickings are better than in their snow-bound upland home. One such we saw at the ranch on a gray November day rooting around on the hillside across the road. Presumably Beautiful's barking annoyed him, for he soon ambled off. We thought that was the last of him—but it wasn't. The bear was joined by another, and the pair broke into an unoccupied summer cabin on the Herb Martyr road a half-mile above us. They caused more havoc than a party of goof-ball delinquents. The front door was smashed in, furniture wrecked, and crockery shattered, while every can was twisted, pried open, and the contents consumed. How the bears managed to use their powerful claws as efficient can-openers I believe would be new to science. The operation might make an interesting study for an ambitious young zoologist seeking a Ph.D.

Old Miguel had the most harrowing experience with a bear in the Chiricahuas since the days of the long-gone grizzlies. He was a swarthy, diminutive Mexican woodcutter who had a Forest Service permit each fall to take out dead oak to fuel his countrymen's stoves and ovens south of the border. This is an established international export business in southern Arizona and will be until some future Great Society provides universal gas and electricity.

Everybody around was acquainted with Miguel; he had been a part of Portal's floating population for as long as people could remember. No one knew his age, including himself, but he looked to be somewhere between ninety-three and one hundred and ten. He was still active and wiry, though, and spent a couple of months every year from dawn to sunset chopping and sawing, packing the wood down to the road on his burro, and stacking it in neat piles for his partner to load on an ancient, dilapidated truck for transport south. Miguel always pitched his ragged tent by the bridge crossing Cave Creek, a half mile below us, opposite the entrance driveway into the Hoskins' place.

"Sit on him!" yelled Chuck.

That did it. Somehow I managed to wrestle a couple of feet of snake under me and held the violently struggling reptile behind the head with both hands. Then together we stuffed the still protesting snake into a bag and securely tied the drawstrings. I was out of breath and felt as if I had tussled with an oversized alligator. But Chuck was not impressed.

"Just routine," he said as he climbed back into the car.

Next I was introduced to the amazing antics of the hog-nosed snake. Chuck spotted one and picked it up in a grassy opening at an elevation of about six thousand feet. This reptile is one of Nature's most accomplished actors, and we decided that a bare spot beside the road would make an excellent movie location for close-ups in the American Museum of Natural History's television series. So Chuck set up the camera, and I dumped the snake out of the canvas bag in front of it.

The reptile immediately flattened its neck and head threateningly, coiled its body, and hissed with the ferocity of the most dreaded of cobras. This was all a complete bluff, as the species is without fangs, poison, or constricting capacity and is comparatively dull. Our specimen, about eighteen inches long, was true to the hog-nosed snake's make-believe theatrical tradition and put on a real show.

Aroused by being poked with a stick, it drew in breath sharply in perfect imitation of a venomous reptile, spread its hood to almost twice normal size, started to strike repeatedly, but never completed the action. Getting nowhere through this impressive exhibition of pugnacity, the snake finally resorted to another

Suddenly it subsided limply, with mouth open, and went into a series of violent convulsions. Then it rolled over on its back and lay still, presumably dead. No amount of prodding or handling revived the snake, and I assumed the act ended on this note of Shakespearean tragedy. But Chuck wasn't finished.

"Turn it over," he directed.

I did, and a surprising thing happened. The reptile came to life, rolled once more on its back, and lay still again in simulated

76

Along about ten o'clock one night a banging on the Hoskins' door brought them both running. Outside stood Miguel. His shirt was torn to tatters, and his left arm was a mass of lacerations.

"Bear come and kill burro," he gasped. "Got in tent and pretty damn near kill me too."

The old Mexican was in great pain and close to complete collapse. The Hoskins got him to a chair and did what they could in the way of first aid. Then they bundled him in the back seat of the car, and Bill raced sixty-five miles to the Douglas hospital. He saw his charge taken care of and didn't get back until 3:30 A.M.

While having a much-needed cup of coffee and sandwich on his return, Bill heard a loud scratching at the kitchen door. He opened it and looked into the face of the bear standing upright with red-stained paws extended. Bruin apparently scented food and was trying to get in for a snack. Bill jumped for his gun and

The Hoskins' bear rug.

shot at the huge black animal through the screen door. The bear dropped on all fours and vanished in the darkness.

"Don't think I killed him," Bill said to his wife. He was correct. After breakfast later that morning the Hoskins found blood in the yard and a trail of crimson spots led off toward the mountains. Bill saddled his horse and took off. In an hour or so he came upon the wounded bear resting. It was somewhat spent from loss of blood, and its breathing was irregular and rasping. But at sight of Bill the bear growled, rose, and gamely tried to do battle. One shot from Bill's rifle put it out of its misery.

"I didn't want to shoot him," said Bill afterwards. "Those bears belong in the Chiricahuas. They've been here a lot longer than we have. If they'd just stay put up in the mountains it's all right with me."

But the Hoskins now have a mighty fine home-grown bear rug in front of their fireplace.

Miguel's indestructible toughness won out and he survived, I'm glad to say. He was back with us the next autumn with another burro he'd picked up somewhere. And the bears still live in the Chiricahua high country, but we never saw another in the canyon.

No, I don't hold with those who say that black bears are harmless to humans. Sometimes they are and sometimes they aren't. Bears are big, and bears are unpredictable. I am very respectful and make no threatening moves when I'm in their territory. But I feel about them as Bill Hoskins does—I'll rise and defend their right to occupy a niche in Arizona's sky islands anytime.

9 *Serpents in Eden*

I have always been able to take snakes or let them alo[ne] until I made a couple of trips with Chuck Bogert. Th[ey] take snakes. Chuck is formally Dr. Charles M. Bogert, the Department of Herpetology at the American Mus[eum of Nat]ural History in New York. Amphibians also com[e] jurisdiction.

A native Californian, he has traveled thousands of [miles collect]ing and studying snakes, lizards, frogs, and toads in t[he] Mexico, and Central America, and recently he went look over the reptile situation there. But his favorit[e are the] Chiricahua Mountains. Almost every summer whil[e at] the Painted Canyon Ranch Chuck, his wife Mickey, [and their] daughters made Portal their headquarters.

Chuck has an unerring eye where snakes and li[zards are con]cerned. A day in the field with him is a lively en[d]cating reptiles and pursuing them over the landsc[ape] trips he travels in a four-wheel-drive station wa[gon] his live specimens in elongated bags of heavy can[vas] section of the car. Whenever the motor is turned [off] the thumping and scratching of the day's catch pullmans."

I found on my first time out that reptile collecti[ng] cut-and-dried affair. We had barely driven two m[iles] jammed on the brakes and nearly catapulted me t[hrough the wind]shield. Like a flash he was out of the car and hold[ing a] five-foot gopher snake.

"Grab him!" he shouted as he threw it onto [the seat be]side me.

I did. But the whole forward part of the car fr[om] seemed to explode with thrashing, twisting snake[s.]

death. Here was a strange flaw in the hog-nosed snake's acting ability for, as often as we repeated the maneuver, it rolled over, belly up, as if it considered this to be the only position suitable to the deceased.

Just what survival value these histrionics have or how they originated, no one knows. But the humbug ferocity of the hog-nosed snake makes it widely feared by humans, especially in the southern United States. There it is known by such awesome names as puff adder, blowing viper, and checkered adder. Actually it is the mildest of reptiles, with a slow-moving, stout, brown body, spotted with large squarish black blotches. It's food consists mostly of toads, frogs, lizards, small mammals, and occasional birds. The upturned snout with its protecting shield, which gives the snake its name, is used to root out reluctant amphibians from the soft soil. We know several people in southern Arizona who keep hog-nosed snakes as pets—docile, gentle, and good mousers, they say. Chuck generously offered me this one. I declined, sure that I could have the hog-nosed snake or Phyllis—not both—and my choice was irrevocably the latter.

One day we went reptile hunting on foot in a rocky, wooded section high up near the Chiricahua divide. We clambered for a mile or so up a rugged gorge, bagging a couple of lizards, but without seeing a sign of a snake. However, as we were about to turn back, Chuck had a final look on a steep-slanting talus slope, and after about a half hour of rough going he came down holding a Price's rattlesnake professionally between his thumb and forefinger. This was a rare find because in the United States the species is restricted to the mountains of southern Arizona. Even there it isn't numerous. Known also as the twin-spotted rattlesnake, it is the smallest of the rattler family, seldom attaining a length of more than two feet. Although an inhabitant of the higher elevations, far above its relatives, this little rattle-tail is so elusive and retiring that I had never seen one before north of the Mexican border in all my mountain wanderings.

In general, snakes play a minor role in the Chiricahua's wildlife show. One may occasionally see a tree-climbing blue racer, king snake, garter snake, or other harmless species, but such horrendous reptilian characters as western diamondback rattlers rarely penetrate farther than the lowest and driest slopes and canyons. But each year a dozen or so are killed by valley ranchers. The formidable-looking stretched skins of the largest, five to six feet long, are usually displayed in the window of the Portal general store; a basket on the counter inside holds a collection of multiple rattles, free for the taking. Sidewinders, too, dwell in the arid, open stretch below Portal. Named because of their odd looping mode of locomotion, these small horned rattlesnakes are dangerous because they are out foraging during the night. Besides rattlesnakes, the only other venomous serpent is the rare red, black, and yellow banded Sonoran coral snake. Its poison is potent and could be deadly. But no one in the Southwest has been bitten so far as I know.

Our own Eden up the canyon wasn't entirely serpentless, but we encountered fewer snakes there than in any other country place we ever lived, East or West. I attribute this scarcity partially to the cats. I never knew any cats to kill a snake or vice versa, but their feline curiosity and keen-eyed vigilance make life uncomfortable for reptiles in their vicinity. This is also true of creeping and crawling varmints of all kinds; we never found a centipede, scorpion, tarantula, or lizard in or around the house. After living many years in the Southwest, we are convinced that no well-organized home in the desert or mountains should be without cats. But maybe this is special pleading because both of us are particularly empathetic where cats are concerned.

However, after four nearly snake-free years, we had a sudden mass invasion of rattlers. Six were killed on the ranch in less than a month—then they were gone. It was during a tinder-dry September after exceptionally light summer rains. Our perennial stream, boggy meadows, pools, and springs provided the only available moisture above ground for miles around. The wild population, large and small, took advantage of our life-giving water-holes, and the rattlers followed their mobile food supply.

The first intimation we had of the unwelcome infestation was an insistent sinister buzzing one morning on the steep, rocky cut across the road from the swimming pool. Nobody has ever been

Along about ten o'clock one night a banging on the Hoskins' door brought them both running. Outside stood Miguel. His shirt was torn to tatters, and his left arm was a mass of lacerations.

"Bear come and kill burro," he gasped. "Got in tent and pretty damn near kill me too."

The old Mexican was in great pain and close to complete collapse. The Hoskins got him to a chair and did what they could in the way of first aid. Then they bundled him in the back seat of the car, and Bill raced sixty-five miles to the Douglas hospital. He saw his charge taken care of and didn't get back until 3:30 A.M.

While having a much-needed cup of coffee and sandwich on his return, Bill heard a loud scratching at the kitchen door. He opened it and looked into the face of the bear standing upright with red-stained paws extended. Bruin apparently scented food and was trying to get in for a snack. Bill jumped for his gun and

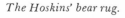
The Hoskins' bear rug.

shot at the huge black animal through the screen door. The bear dropped on all fours and vanished in the darkness.

"Don't think I killed him," Bill said to his wife. He was correct. After breakfast later that morning the Hoskins found blood in the yard and a trail of crimson spots led off toward the mountains. Bill saddled his horse and took off. In an hour or so he came upon the wounded bear resting. It was somewhat spent from loss of blood, and its breathing was irregular and rasping. But at sight of Bill the bear growled, rose, and gamely tried to do battle. One shot from Bill's rifle put it out of its misery.

"I didn't want to shoot him," said Bill afterwards. "Those bears belong in the Chiricahuas. They've been here a lot longer than we have. If they'd just stay put up in the mountains it's all right with me."

But the Hoskins now have a mighty fine home-grown bear rug in front of their fireplace.

Miguel's indestructible toughness won out and he survived, I'm glad to say. He was back with us the next autumn with another burro he'd picked up somewhere. And the bears still live in the Chiricahua high country, but we never saw another in the canyon.

No, I don't hold with those who say that black bears are harmless to humans. Sometimes they are and sometimes they aren't. Bears are big, and bears are unpredictable. I am very respectful and make no threatening moves when I'm in their territory. But I feel about them as Bill Hoskins does—I'll rise and defend their right to occupy a niche in Arizona's sky islands anytime.

9 *Serpents in Eden*

I have always been able to take snakes or let them alone. That is, until I made a couple of trips with Chuck Bogert. Then I had to take snakes. Chuck is formally Dr. Charles M. Bogert, Director of the Department of Herpetology at the American Museum of Natural History in New York. Amphibians also come under his jurisdiction.

A native Californian, he has traveled thousands of miles collecting and studying snakes, lizards, frogs, and toads in the Southwest, Mexico, and Central America, and recently he went to Ceylon to look over the reptile situation there. But his favorite haunt is the Chiricahua Mountains. Almost every summer while we were at the Painted Canyon Ranch Chuck, his wife Mickey, and their two daughters made Portal their headquarters.

Chuck has an unerring eye where snakes and lizards are concerned. A day in the field with him is a lively endurance test locating reptiles and pursuing them over the landscape. On longer trips he travels in a four-wheel-drive station wagon and stores his live specimens in elongated bags of heavy canvas in the rear section of the car. Whenever the motor is turned off one can hear the thumping and scratching of the day's catch in their "snake pullmans."

I found on my first time out that reptile collecting is no prosaic, cut-and-dried affair. We had barely driven two miles when Chuck jammed on the brakes and nearly catapulted me through the windshield. Like a flash he was out of the car and holding up a writhing five-foot gopher snake.

"Grab him!" he shouted as he threw it onto the front seat beside me.

I did. But the whole forward part of the car from floor to ceiling seemed to explode with thrashing, twisting snake.

"Sit on him!" yelled Chuck.

That did it. Somehow I managed to wrestle a couple of feet of snake under me and held the violently struggling reptile behind the head with both hands. Then together we stuffed the still protesting snake into a bag and securely tied the drawstrings. I was out of breath and felt as if I had tussled with an oversized alligator. But Chuck was not impressed.

"Just routine," he said as he climbed back into the car.

Next I was introduced to the amazing antics of the hog-nosed snake. Chuck spotted one and picked it up in a grassy opening at an elevation of about six thousand feet. This reptile is one of Nature's most accomplished actors, and we decided that a bare spot beside the road would make an excellent movie location for close-ups in the American Museum of Natural History's television series. So Chuck set up the camera, and I dumped the snake out of the canvas bag in front of it.

The reptile immediately flattened its neck and head threateningly, coiled its body, and hissed with the ferocity of the most dreaded of cobras. This was all a complete bluff, as the species is without fangs, poison, or constricting capacity and is comparatively small. Our specimen, about eighteen inches long, was true to the hog-nosed snake's make-believe theatrical tradition and put on a good show.

Aroused by being poked with a stick, it drew in breath sharply in perfect imitation of a venomous reptile, spread its hood to almost twice normal size, started to strike repeatedly, but never completed the action. Getting nowhere through this impressive exhibition of pugnacity, the snake finally resorted to another trick.

Suddenly it subsided limply, with mouth open, and went into a series of violent convulsions. Then it rolled over on its back and lay still, presumably dead. No amount of prodding or handling roused the snake, and I assumed the act ended on this note of Shakespearean tragedy. But Chuck wasn't finished.

"Turn it over," he directed.

I did, and a surprising thing happened. The reptile came to life, rolled once more on its back, and lay still again in simulated death. Here was a strange flaw in the hog-nosed snake's acting ability for, as often as we repeated the maneuver, it rolled over, belly up, as if it considered this to be the only position suitable to the deceased.

Just what survival value these histrionics have or how they originated, no one knows. But the humbug ferocity of the hog-nosed snake makes it widely feared by humans, especially in the southern United States. There it is known by such awesome names as puff adder, blowing viper, and checkered adder. Actually it is the mildest of reptiles, with a slow-moving, stout, brown body, spotted with large squarish black blotches. It's food consists mostly of toads, frogs, lizards, small mammals, and occasional birds. The upturned snout with its protecting shield, which gives the snake its name, is used to root out reluctant amphibians from the soft soil. We know several people in southern Arizona who keep hog-nosed snakes as pets—docile, gentle, and good mousers, they say. Chuck generously offered me this one. I declined, sure that I could have the hog-nosed snake or Phyllis—not both—and my choice was irrevocably the latter.

One day we went reptile hunting on foot in a rocky, wooded section high up near the Chiricahua divide. We clambered for a mile or so up a rugged gorge, bagging a couple of lizards, but without seeing a sign of a snake. However, as we were about to turn back, Chuck had a final look on a steep-slanting talus slope, and after about a half hour of rough going he came down holding a Price's rattlesnake professionally between his thumb and forefinger. This was a rare find because in the United States the species is restricted to the mountains of southern Arizona. Even there it isn't numerous. Known also as the twin-spotted rattlesnake, it is the smallest of the rattler family, seldom attaining a length of more than two feet. Although an inhabitant of the higher elevations, far above its relatives, this little rattle-tail is so elusive and retiring that I had never seen one before north of the Mexican border in all my mountain wanderings.

In general, snakes play a minor role in the Chiricahua's wildlife show. One may occasionally see a tree-climbing blue racer, king snake, garter snake, or other harmless species, but such horrendous reptilian characters as western diamondback rattlers rarely penetrate farther than the lowest and driest slopes and canyons. But each year a dozen or so are killed by valley ranchers. The formidable-looking stretched skins of the largest, five to six feet long, are usually displayed in the window of the Portal general store; a basket on the counter inside holds a collection of multiple rattles, free for the taking. Sidewinders, too, dwell in the arid, open stretch below Portal. Named because of their odd looping mode of locomotion, these small horned rattlesnakes are dangerous because they are out foraging during the night. Besides rattlesnakes, the only other venomous serpent is the rare red, black, and yellow banded Sonoran coral snake. Its poison is potent and could be deadly. But no one in the Southwest has been bitten so far as I know.

Our own Eden up the canyon wasn't entirely serpentless, but we encountered fewer snakes there than in any other country place we ever lived, East or West. I attribute this scarcity partially to the cats. I never knew any cats to kill a snake or vice versa, but their feline curiosity and keen-eyed vigilance make life uncomfortable for reptiles in their vicinity. This is also true of creeping and crawling varmints of all kinds; we never found a centipede, scorpion, tarantula, or lizard in or around the house. After living many years in the Southwest, we are convinced that no well-organized home in the desert or mountains should be without cats. But maybe this is special pleading because both of us are particularly empathetic where cats are concerned.

However, after four nearly snake-free years, we had a sudden mass invasion of rattlers. Six were killed on the ranch in less than a month—then they were gone. It was during a tinder-dry September after exceptionally light summer rains. Our perennial stream, boggy meadows, pools, and springs provided the only available moisture above ground for miles around. The wild population, large and small, took advantage of our life-giving water-holes, and the rattlers followed their mobile food supply.

The first intimation we had of the unwelcome infestation was an insistent sinister buzzing one morning on the steep, rocky cut across the road from the swimming pool. Nobody has ever been able to describe the sound, but a rattler's penetrating z-z-z-z-z is unmistakable even to those who have never heard it before. On the hottest day it can send a chill up and down the spinal column. We hurried to the pool and looked up. There, facing each other among the boulders, were Whitey and a good-sized diamondback engaged in earnest combat. The rattler was coiled, its vibrating tail erect, and head raised menacingly. Whitey crouched facing her adversary, hair bristling. The snake struck again and again. Each time the cat ducked, just escaping the poison fangs, and retaliated in a series of lightning swift cuffs with bared claws. Back and forth went the thrusts, feints, and ripostes, while we looked on in almost hypnotic fascination.

After a few minutes we sensed a subtle change in the battle. The snake, still coiled and rattling, began a slow backward retreat, and Whitey was cautiously advancing. Finally, the reptile reached a protecting rock, uncoiled, and ignominiously slithered away up the hillside. All was quiet. The cat carefully descended the slope, crossed the road to us, and rubbed against our legs.

"Good stuff, Whitey," I said.

A contented purr was the answer.

Next it was Barney's excited yowling a day or two later which warned us of another rattler in the woodpile beside the house. But the climax came, ironically enough, after I had left on a two-weeks' reptile collecting trip with Chuck Bogert in Mexico's Sierra Madre Occidental. That was the time Phyllis literally jumped out of her shoes. In bathing suit and loose beach slippers, she was about to take an afternoon dip in the pool but decided first to check on one of the rabbits who was about to have a litter of babies.

We had brought a half dozen rabbits and a flock of chickens from the Flying H Ranch. The bunnies were installed in roomy cages on three-foot legs under the walnut tree by the Reed cabin. The expectant mother rabbit had pulled fur from her body and padded the nesting box at the rear of the cage with the soft, warm insulation. Phyllis lifted the lid on the nest to see if the young had arrived. They hadn't. But like a jack-in-the-box, a rattler's head rose up before her adorned with a blob of white rabbit fur, like an old man with bushy whiskers. Phyllis dropped the lid as if it were red hot, then saw a second rattlesnake just below the cage at her feet. The next thing she remembers is being back at the house barefoot, the bathing slippers remaining side by side beneath the rabbit hutch. Nothing would induce her to go back, but fortunately Len Banks was on hand to dispatch the snakes and retrieve the abandoned footwear.

When Chuck and I returned, Phyllis asked if we'd seen any.

"Only a couple of little fellows on the rim of the Barranca Del Cobre."

"Well, we did!" she said with what I thought unwonted vehemence. That was the last close brush we had with rattlers at Painted Canyon Ranch.

Although Phyllis's violent antipathy to snakes is understandable, I never shared the feeling. Rather, I felt it was a privilege to learn from Chuck something of the lives, habits, and mysterious mechanisms of these remarkable creatures. Underlying all of his meticulous gathering of material, I believe, is an ambition to produce a definitive general biology of reptiles. That he is capable of accomplishing such a herculean task is foreshadowed by his *The Gila Monster And Its Allies,* which Chuck wrote with Rafael Martin del Campo of the National University of Mexico.

This impressive monograph about the poisonous orange and black beaded lizard of our Southwestern deserts and its blue and black relative south of the border took many years of painstaking research in the field and laboratory, and is the authoritative work on the subject.

My copy is inscribed by the author: "For Weldon Heald, who tolerates herpetologists as well as gila monsters." However, I cannot honestly say that Chuck Bogert made a snake fancier out of me. But toleration is a mild word for the deep respect I have for both reptiles and those who spend their lives studying them.

10 *Unusual Guests*

As a teen-ager, about a hundred years ago, I lived in a little southern New Hampshire town. All around were wooded hills, upland fields, and a scattering of steel-bright ponds. Summer, winter, spring, and fall, whenever opportunity offered, I escaped from arduous juvenile duties to explore the countryside, and in time acquired a fair amount of woodcraft and nature lore. Daniel Boone was my hero. In his image I wore a coonskin cap and carried a .22-caliber rifle in the crook of my arm. Then one day with accidental accuracy I shot a squirrel out of the top of a tall pine. He was kicking and chattering when he hit the ground, and I had to finish him off with the butt of my rifle. It was then I discovered what H. L. Mencken called "the armed pursuit of the lower fauna" was not for me. So, in spite of Daniel Boone, I sold the rifle and have never carried one since, except for my stint in the army during World War II.

The difference was immediately noticeable. The wild creatures seemed to sense I was no longer a foe and were little disturbed by my peaceful intrusions into their affairs. With a gun I had caught sight of few animals except flashes of those in hurried retreat. But unarmed I saw for the first time the shorttail weasel and snowshoe hare in white winter coats, observed raccoons catching fish in a shallow stream, and watched a family party of otters disport themselves by repeatedly sliding down a steep mudbank and splashing into a pond. I looked in on the busy doings of a dozen kinds of animals I'd never seen before. They didn't seem to mind.

Among the birds and beasts, it seems to me, fear of humans has been brought about solely by Man himself. He is responsible for the extinction or near extinction of some forty species of North American mammals and birds; the decimation of wildlife throughout the world is almost beyond belief. But people who live in a relatively natural habitat, as Phyllis and I did at Painted Canyon Ranch, soon learn that there is little innate fear of humans among animals, nor does there appear to be much antagonism. Quite the reverse. When we showed ourselves as beings of good will, distrust vanished, and many formerly furtive and timid creatures actually appeared willing to give up their way of life and accept the security of our friendship, the abundant hand-outs, and comfortable accommodations.

In describing animals, scientists eschew what they term the "pathetic fallacy." By that they mean our tendency to endow other forms of life with human traits and feelings. Thus, specialists limit their descriptions of animal behavior to purely mechanical reactions. Such words as malice, hate, love, jealousy, joy, sorrow, sympathy, and gratitude are taboo. All is put on a dead level of verifiable fact.

But a scientific inventory of an animal's physical makeup and habits often fails to portray its character and personality. All living beings are unique, both individually and generically, and their endowments add up to much more than length, breadth, dental formulas, number of bones, and means of subsistence. Only by borrowing from the lexicon of human emotions can one describe the true nature of an animal.

Our wild neighbors who dropped in to see us were presumably unaware of the "pathetic fallacy." Their actions were similar to those of human beings, and we could easily tell when they were pleased, disappointed, expectant, curious, frustrated, or confused. Granted there is a vast difference between the tropisms of an amoeba and the cerebrations of an Einstein. But just what point on the evolutionary ladder conditioned reflexes become thought is debatable. Some scientists would have us believe a definite distinction exists between the mental processes of human beings and all other animals. But I believe this is arbitrary and that there is a descending scale from the highest to the lowest with few gaps or breaks. The behavior patterns of organisms seem to be due to varying degrees of complexity rather than to differences in kind.

After many years of observing animals from a layman's point of view, I would say that determination is the dominating driving force which animates all living beings. It is evident throughout, from unicellular organisms to Man, and underlies the majority of all their activities. Even a ladybug shows strong signs of determination. I've often tried to deter one from going in the direction it has chosen. But no matter how often I blocked the route or turned the little insect around, it still persisted in its original course. If thwarted long enough, the ladybug gives every evidence of petulant irritation, but it doesn't capitulate or retreat.

So perhaps when determination becomes conscious and selective, thought is born. At that point an organism's behavior is directed by mental as well as physical and mechanical processes. If so, I believe this brain-directed determination occurs at a level far below that of Man. Of course, I could be wrong—but so could the scientists. They often are.

Although our animal guests differed greatly in size, shape, habits, and temperaments, one trait they had in common. That was a craving for affection. This appears to be another basic urge in living beings, and was exhibited by such a lowly creature as the horned toad who dwelt in our stone wall. The appealing miniature dragon closed its eyes and relaxed when we picked him up and stroked his head with our fingers. The benefits of freedom and independence are stressed in philosophy and often in politics. But it is apparently a relatively recent human concept. The wild, soaring flight of an eagle is given symbolic significance. But it is our conviction that most animals will exchange this much vaunted freedom for affection, approbation, and security. A goodly part of the world's human population seems so inclined too.

This all-powerful craving is being increasingly recognized and it has completely altered the techniques of handling performing animals. What is called affection-training has supplanted the former whip-and-chair tactics. Trainers have become understanding "mother substitutes" who chuck lions under the chin, stroke tigers, and whisper love words into elephants' oversize ears. Bruno, the bear, drinks soda pop, while Judy, the chimp, has a chocolate-covered doughnut and a cup of half-and-half coffee for breakfast every morning. With such sympathetic treatment animals become happy and secure and don't want to leave.

The revolutionary about-face in our attitude toward animals is reflected in such popular books as *Born Free* and *Ring of Bright Water,* and the television series "Wild Kingdom" and "Daktari." Perhaps the most encouraging evidence of a better understanding of the non-human world and its importance is in children's education. Recently I looked over a new juvenile book titled *Wild Animal Pets.* Profusely illustrated with color photographs, it graphically shows the possibilities among insects, amphibians, reptiles and mammals. The text describes the different animals' habits and requirements, how to build homes for them, what to feed them, and their general care. Never once does the author suggest involuntary captivity or close confinement. I don't know the children's reaction to this book, but mine was enthusiastic. I was all for bringing Phyllis home a couple of skinks (Sic!) .

There is no question that many wild animals can be desirable pets. They are usually docile, good natured, and in time affectionate. The Healys over in the Huachucas had a coati that slept on a blanket in a corner of the porch and loved to romp with the dog. The Sharps, up near Globe, took in a young peccary who became a member of the family. "Pecky" chewed gum constantly between meals, and every evening chomped onto the end of a burlap sack and engaged in a vigorous tug-of-war with Joe Sharp round and round the living room. The Bogerts raised several wildcats from kittens, and the kitchen of the Coronado Ranch, on the other side of the mountains, was home to a porcupine for a considerable spell.

We preferred to think of our own animal callers as guests rather than pets. They came unannounced and left when they felt like it. Phyllis and I enjoyed their visits, though, and they were always welcome to return. We hadn't been at Painted Canyon Ranch a month when the first one arrived.

Callers were generally greeted by Beautiful's excited barking. At dusk one late November afternoon we knew by her staccato yelps that a visitor of particular note must have arrived at the back door. This is standard procedure, as no one ever comes to the front door at a dyed-in-the-wool Arizona ranch. So we donned welcoming smiles, lit the coffee burner, and turned the light on outside the kitchen. Apparently, however, there was nothing there except the three cats having their evening meal around a big pan of milk, heads down and tails straight up.

Suddenly both Phyllis and I did an incredulous double take. In the triangle of cats' tails rose a beautiful plumy white brush which was attached to an animal with gleaming white back and coal-black undersides. Our unexpected guest was a hog-nosed skunk, so called because of his upturned, pig-like snout. This is a Central- and South-American species that ranges into the southwestern United States, and is one of the handsomest of the whole skunk clan.

"Weldon," sissy wildcat.

The cats seemed completely unconcerned about their strange dinner companion, and the skunk greedily drank the milk, paying not the slightest attention to them or to Beautiful who continued to bark at a respectful distance.

Milk finished, the cats licked their chops and began washing themselves, while the skunk wandered among them on a leisurely tour of inspection. Then he sedately took his leave and slowly ambled off into the gathering darkness. We turned off the light, believing we had seen something unique—the skunk who came to dinner.

But next morning he appeared again for a hearty breakfast, and from then on throughout the winter he was our house guest. He ate with the cats, played with the cats, and contentedly dozed in the sun with the cats. Phyllis and I are sure he thought he was a cat. His lengthy stay wasn't marred by one unpleasant incident. He didn't bother the chickens, and not once was the noxious skunk odor perceptible. We found this much-maligned animal to be scrupulously clean, polite, and mild mannered, and his appealing

Beautiful tries to play with a chipmunk.

personality and exemplary habits made cats, humans, and even Beautiful accept him as one of the family. However, several of our friends beat startled retreats until they got used to running across a skunk in our yard or on the front porch.

These were his favorite places and when not on solemn inspections of the grounds, he slept under the dog's bed on the veranda. In time our friendly skunk visitor came when we called him, followed us on chores, took food from our hands, and loved to be stroked, patted on the head, and scratched behind the ears. Then he would show his appreciation of our hospitality by nuzzling our hands and rubbing against our legs much as a house tabby does. Most of all, though, he seemed to enjoy sitting in Phyllis's lap, snuggling up under her chin.

One day in March we heard Beautiful's excited yelping once more. She led us to the meadow beyond the creek where our skunk lay dead. There were no marks of violence, nor strong musky smell, and we concluded that he had been a victim of the mysterious malady that periodically attacks our wildlife.

We buried our skunk under a big cottonwood tree beside the stream, and both of us were affected by the loss of this likeable little animal. We missed him. I never thought I'd see the day when my wife would shed a tear—for a skunk!

Our acquaintance with bats wasn't voluntary. We shared the general revulsion humans have for these harmless and beneficial aerial mammals. But there are some twenty species of bats in the Chiricahuas, and it was inevitable that we should meet. Every day at dusk during the warm season, dark, flying shapes materialized out of nowhere and fluttered back and forth the length of the swimming pool. These were bats having a preliminary drink before their night-long meal on some of the Chiricahuas' twenty thousand different kinds of insects. Dozens of them would crisscross over the water, lightly touching the surface for a split second as they scooped up a few drops. This lasted fifteen or twenty minutes. Then they went their ways, and we were usually bat-free until the next evening's drinking bout.

But not always. We left doors and windows open before we made part of the veranda a screened porch, and the first summer the house was patrolled almost every night by a couple of Mexican freetail bats. One took an outside beat in front of the veranda, while the other's route was close under the veranda roof, with a regularly scheduled detour through the living room and adjacent master bedroom about every ten minutes. They were fully as efficient as fly screens, and insects miraculously disappeared as the bats passed by. Not even a mosquito buzzed in our ears as we slept, and in the morning the bats were gone. Far from familiarity breeding contempt, the two freetails gained our profound respect and made us marvel that Nature could devise any creature as wonderful as a bat. However, we never became fond of our freetails. A live-and-let-live attitude was the best we could achieve.

A poser is the bats' uncanny ability to navigate in complete darkness. Tests have demonstrated that they can fly rapidly, wheeling and twisting for hours at a time in a totally blacked-out room and never come in contact with a closely strung network of wires.

Shut a bat's eyes with glue and he will fly with greater assurance than with his eyes open; close his ears and he will bump into obstacles. But the saying "blind as a bat" is unfounded, for they have excellent sight in semi-darkness and only a mild case of astigmatism in full sunlight. Also it is highly improbable that a bat ever became entangled in a lady's hair—or if one did, it must have been a most unusual occasion.

Authorities now seem pretty well agreed that bats operate a sort of acoustical "sonar" system by emitting short, high-pitched squeaks, listening for the echoes, and accurately avoiding the obstructions which produce them. Presumably a different sort of echo locates the exact position of an edible flying insect. The high-speed supersonic squeaks, chittering, humming, or whatever sounds a bat makes to insure safe maneuvering are far beyond the range of the human ear. To us the freetails' night patrols were completely noiseless. Other specialists, however, attribute the whole operation to "the muscle memory of the kinesthetic sense." This classifies bats as sort of flying IBM machines.

But ours didn't always follow the dictum of science to the letter. If a door or window was unexpectedly closed or a temporary obstacle forced the bats to vary their routes, they appeared to become baffled and banged into walls and thumped the ceiling in apparently annoyed frustration. Meanwhile they seemed unaware of other exits and entrances within a few feet of their accustomed flight.

Bats belong to an order not even remotely related to any other, and they are the only mammals capable of true flight. There are, in fact, so many mysterious anomalies about these weird, unbelievable animals that myths and legends have given them the reputation of being malevolent visitors from the nether regions. Most people shudder at the mere mention of bats, and they are generally considered to be unclean, evil, repulsive creatures, fit consorts of vampires, werewolves, and witches. But never has an animal been more slandered, and almost every popular story about the maliciousness of bats is plain libel. Their chief value to mankind is as allies in the never-ending battle to keep the world from being taken over by the insects. Bat metropolis of the Southwest is

One of the many caves in the walls of Cave Creek Canyon.

Carlsbad Caverns in southern New Mexico. There in prosperous times three million fly-by-nights of five species issue forth each evening and consume twelve tons of moths, beetles, flies, and other insects before morning. They are said to eat half their weight every twenty-four hours.

We were fairly sure that our freetails domiciled with a bat colony in Crystal Cave. There, with hundreds of others, they slept the days away hanging upside down from the ceiling by their sharp, rear toenails, wings folded about them like closed umbrellas. Crystal Cave is a limestone cavern located on National Forest land about a half mile west of the ranch. Once well-known locally as Forest Cave, it is the reason for the name Cave Creek, and was formerly often visited. The cavern consists of a maze of passages, corridors, halls, and domed rooms, decorated with carbonated lime formations, sparkling crystal deposits, and icicle-like stalactites. The insignificant entrance, however, is well hidden and hard to find, so few people now know about the cave. When asked, we gave visitors rather vague directions, as there has been considerable vandalism.

A dynamic young man of the executive, attaché-case type called on us regarding Crystal Cave. Over bourbon-on-the-rocks he told us how we could clean up. He was speaking financially. The proposition was to obtain a Forest Service special-use permit and develop the cave as a tourist attraction. For an investment of thirty thousand dollars on our part he would adequately light the cavern, construct safe black-topped paths, and install all other necessary improvements. The youthful promoter would then manage the concession for half the take. His enthusiasm was catching, but we reluctantly declined. Our negative answer was not based solely on the fact that such a project would disturb our freetails' home.

I'm certain, however, that had we wanted to capitalize on the trust and friendship of our animal neighbors, Phyllis and I could have assembled a remarkable collection of regional wildlife that people would have come far to see.

11 *The Four Seasons*

Southeastern Arizona is a climatic paradox. Right in the middle of North America's driest and hottest deserts, Nature plumped a roomy oasis of ten thousand square miles. Here along the Mexican border are places where summers are cooler than the Middle West, yet January is as balmy as central Georgia or Mississippi.

This natural air-conditioning trick is achieved by boosting the whole region into the sky where it receives a unique combination of cool breezes in summer and a warm winter sun. Unlike the low central and western part of the state, Arizona's southeastern corner is high; fully eighty per cent is above 4,000 feet and much of it is 1,000 feet more.

In this paradoxical oasis Nature went to work and carved out broad, sweeping valleys, rolling plateaus, and long, swelling mountain ranges to the blue horizon, a hundred miles away. Over the hills she spread a carpet of grass for thousands of cattle to graze, and buried treasures of gold, silver, and copper for men to dig up. To finish it off she scattered oak groves here and there and clothed the lofty, sky-island archipelago with five hundred square miles of evergreen forests that look as if they had been stolen from northern Idaho.

But Nature skimped on water and she left a landscape vast, harsh, and rough-hewn. It is a region in which people can live, work, and play, but with a special set of rules that have to be learned if one would succeed. Nobody yet has been able to smooth out the ragged edges and tame the country.

Although unusual, southeastern Arizona's mixed brands of weather aren't accidental. The area's position on the continent makes its peculiar climate inevitable. With cosmic simplicity, the year is divided into two totally different regimes, drawing air masses from sources thousands of miles apart. Winter weather originates on the north Pacific Ocean in the Gulf of Alaska, while summer rains and temperatures are manufactured locally with an assist from the far-off Atlantic.

From November to April precipitation comes from remnants of West Coast storms, which have had a large part of their moisture wrung out of them by California's mountain ramparts. If the Pacific storm track is farther south than usual, Arizona's winter rains are fairly generous. But when the annual cold-season parade of low-pressure areas passes inland well to the north, little moisture results. Then the winter may be almost rainless, as are normally spring and fall.

By early summer the Aleutian "weather factory" goes out of business. Low pressure is replaced by a huge, semi-permanent high-pressure area over the north Pacific which persists until fall. Storm production stops, California goes dry, and no moisture is available to Arizona from that direction. But by a remarkable reversal of terrestrial thermodynamics, the interior Southwest finds a different supply of moisture during the hot season which produces sixty to seventy per cent of the entire annual precipitation. This is a sub-continent monsoonal action caused by rapidly rising air over the sun-heated earth which creates a partial vacuum. This pulls in a moist atmospheric "tongue" all the way from the Gulf of Mexico. The combination of ascending air and imported water vapor triggers daily convection showers accompanied by thunder and lightning.

Nowhere have I seen such grand, crashing, sky-filling thunder storms as break over the country from late June to mid-September. To me, these prodigious afternoon and evening deluges are one of Nature's top sights, unrivalled for the kaleidoscopic drama of ever-changing form, color, motion, and vital, unleashed power. But amid blinding flashes of lightning and the almost continuous deafening roar of thunder, these storms can be somewhat too awe-inspiring for comfort on the high summits and exposed ridges of the Chiricahuas. Fire towers and cabins are all carefully grounded and the lookouts ride out these terrifying celestial bombing raids in their insulated havens, while hissing sparks shoot along their

telephone lines, metal hums and crackles, and the lookouts' hair literally stands on end.

Throughout the mountains are evidences of the annual summer bombardment from the skies. Hundreds of trees are struck and fused rocks show where thunderbolts have melted solid stone. As everywhere, lightning plays freakish pranks and no two strikes are identical. Ponderosa pines and Douglas firs are the favorite victims, while white firs, Engelmann spruce, and aspen are seldom touched. The tops of pines are usually blasted off and deep, straight grooves are gouged down the trunks to the ground, but the bark of Douglas firs is ripped off in a spiral furrow, a foot or two wide, often circling the tree five or six times. I ran across one huge Douglas fir, 150 feet tall and eight feet in diameter, which had been struck twice; one spiral groove, bright and new, alternated with an older gray furrow in a startling barber-pole effect. But the wounded veteran lived on.

During a particularly violent July storm, I saw a capricious bolt split just below the summit of Flys Peak and simultaneously strike a row of three majestic pines. It left similar grooves in each as if meticulously measured with a precision instrument. Some trees, however, when hit seem to explode, throwing bark and chunks of torn wood a hundred feet in all directions. And so, although I found these tumultuous storms one of the most fascinating features of our sky island, I preferred to do my on-the-spot investigating after they had passed.

Fortunately dry lightning is rare. The three forest fires that occured while we lived in the Chiricahuas started from other causes —two of them were man-made. Actually, I never saw lightning set a live tree ablaze, though often after a storm we spotted a column or two of smoke rising from dead snags in the upper forests. But the super-saturated vegetation was fireproof, and the next storm usually doused the last sparks.

None of the structures at Painted Canyon Ranch were hit, but we had some close calls and near misses. The one I remember best happened on an August afternoon while a Michigan couple were calling on us. We were having a round of coffee and cake on the screened porch, enjoying a refreshing shower.

"Doesn't everything smell good in the rain?" said Phyllis, inhaling deeply.

BANG!

The conversation was interrupted by a brilliant flash and ear-splitting detonation as a bolt of lightning struck a Chihuahua pine a hundred yards up the road. The Michigan lady's half-full cup flew into the air and landed with a crash on the cement floor, ten feet away. However, that was the only lightning damage we ever suffered.

Cumulous clouds, trailing curtains of rain.

The summer rainy season has few gray, drippy days. Although sometimes violent, the storms are usually of small extent, and they move across the country on unpredictable courses, often producing a cloudburst in one creek-bed and skipping an adjacent watershed entirely. A July or August morning may dawn cloudless. Then around 9:00 A.M. puffy little white wisps appear over the mountains. These expand and coalesce until by mid-afternoon gigantic cumuli boil thousands of feet upward. Sometimes one can count as many as ten separate storms, near and far, in a grand, elemental spectacle, accompanied by pyrotechnic lightning flashes, rolling thunder, and high-arched rainbows. Yet by 10:00 P.M. the stars may be twinkling in a clear, black-velvet sky. The odds of getting wet on a particular day are about fifty-fifty, but torrential rains of short duration may be expected anywhere at any time during the summer. And the transition from no water to too much water can be sudden and sometimes dangerous.

It happened to us—once. We were returning from a shopping trip to Douglas, and the afternoon storms were especially impressive. Several were working on the Peloncillos, to the east, and an enormous thunderhead towered over the Chiricahuas. Our mountains looked as if they were getting a real "duck-drowner." But there was no rain in the valley. The first intimation we had of unusual happenings was when we drove over the Cave Creek bridge into Portal. The stream was a raging river overflowing its banks and flooding the adjacent low spots with a couple of feet of swirling water.

"Big cloudburst in the hills," they told us at the Post Office. "Almost washed your place away and the swimming pool is full of rocks."

"Let's go," I said. And we did.

The storm had passed, but as we drove up Cave Creek Canyon the walls were shedding water as if they had just been raised from the sea. Everywhere the rocks were white-threaded with a network of descending rills, and dozens of cascades and waterfalls poured over the cliffs. In several places the road was under water, and the rushing creek was within a couple of inches of the South Fork bridge timbers. We wondered if there would be anything left of Painted Canyon Ranch.

There was. Turning the last corner, we saw that the buildings still stood. But the yard looked as if a couple of bulldozers had played tag there. The usually dry branch of the creek beside the house had become the sluice for a rampaging flood which overflowed, tearing out the lower part of the lawn and filling the pool brim-full of muddy water. The same runaway stream had jumped its banks above and sent a sizable spate down the driveway into the kitchen and dining room. As Phyllis well observed, things were a mess.

With the aid of Len and Irma Banks, we shoveled, swept, and mopped up the water and silt in the house. However, cleaning out the pool was a tremendous job. Fortunately the report of "rocks in the pool" was an exaggeration. But when the water was drained with a gasoline pump, we found two to three feet of solid mud and sand at the bottom. I labored with two itinerant Mexicans more than a month before the pool was fit to use again. In compensation Phyllis's and my Spanish improved considerably, as the swarthy pair spoke no English.

Such inundations are rare and are usually referred to by Arizonans as "fifty-year floods." We estimated that this exceptional downpour dumped at least four inches of rain in a concentrated area above us in less than an hour, and the runoff funelled through

Our winters were delightful, too.

the ranch to the narrow upper entrance of Cave Creek Canyon. It didn't happen again, and in general the summers at our mountain home were the pleasantest we ever experienced anywhere. I must admit, however, that we added another foot to the height of our retaining wall and kept a wary weather eye out when storms sent hurrying, temporary streams down the creek bed by the house.

Our winters were delightful, too. Night temperatures generally fell below freezing, but day would follow day crisp, clear, and sparkling, as long as two weeks at a stretch. Winter weather at Painted Canyon Ranch resembled the bright, golden autumns of the northern states. Moderate rains came occasionally, and four or five times a year snow transformed our surroundings with white magic, but the warm sun usually returned the landscape to normal within twenty-four hours. Eight inches was our greatest snowfall. However, all winter long the Chiricahua divide behind us glittered with a snowcap several feet deep, and I have encountered

The pool, fed by a warm spring (72° F.), never freezes.

small, hard-frozen patches on the north side of the highest peaks as late as mid-June.

Though as a rule the cold spells last only a day or two, winter as well as summer had its exceptions. Arctic air masses follow Pacific storms across the Southwest, sending the temperatures plummeting. Once after a six-inch snowfall we recorded five degrees below zero at the ranch. No old-timer could remember anything like it for forty years, and Chiricahuans still talk about the night of the Big Freeze.

I was maintaining bachelor's quarters at the time: Phyllis was in California and the Banks weren't with us. The snow stopped around 5:00 P.M. and the mercury in the thermometer by the kitchen door started a spectacular dive. I drained the water pump and the pipes in the house. Even with the heat going full-blast and extra logs in the fireplace, it was chilly indoors at bedtime. Piling on the covers I retreated beneath them for the night. Just before dawn a sharp report like a rifle shot startled me wide awake and on my feet in the middle of the room. Shivering in the icy atmosphere, I investigated and discovered that the wash basin in the bathroom had sprung six inches from the wall, pulling the pipes out with it and splitting the tile floor. Later I found that the pump outside had cracked. Apparently enough water remained in the pipes to do the damage. Until the pump was soldered at the machine shop in Douglas and the plumbing repaired, my water supply came in pails from the spring in the front yard.

The road over the Chiricahuas crosses Onion Saddle on the divide at an elevation of 7,600 feet, and winter snows often make the route impassable. When this occurred we were supposed to put up a warning at the Herb Martyr turn, just above us. But somebody had lost the sign long ago, and the forest ranger never furnished us with a replacement. The result was that each winter some innocent motorists were stranded. Several times we went up as far as we could drive and rescued California school teachers, Iowa farmers, and assorted winter tourists.

One cold, rainy afternoon Phyllis and I, with Beautiful and the cats, were sitting snugly before the warm fire. Suddenly three sodden apparitions passed by the side window. We knew them for outlanders because they knocked at the front door. It was a man and two women. We asked them in, and as they shed their wet wraps, they introduced themselves in varying degrees of broken English. Phyllis recognized the man's name as that of a Swiss designer and manufacturer of women's sport clothes. With him was his Dutch mother, well over seventy years old, and a French lady of uncertain age. They were driving across the country bound for the Pacific Coast, and had taken our back road because it appealed to them on the map. The rear wheels of their car had skidded in the snow over the edge of a sharp turn just below the saddle and bogged down. The three had walked the seven miles back, first through snow, then rain.

We sat them before the fireplace where they gradually revived over cup after cup of hot tea. Then I phoned the manager of the AVA Ranch in Portal who arrived a half hour later with his truck and two helpers. I hopped aboard, and we pushed up through to the immobilized car. By then it was pitch-dark. With the aid of the truck's headlights, the four of us worked amidst the swirling snowflakes with a block-and-tackle. But with every inch gained pulling up the front wheels, the car's rear end slipped farther down over the edge. After an hour and a half we gave up. Another try was made next day, but the truck was stopped by a foot of snow a mile below the stranded automobile.

It was the Swiss gentleman's turn. He called a garage in Douglas and made a sporting proposition—sixty dollars if they extricated his car, nothing if they couldn't. It was accepted. We admired his business acumen and could understand why he was successful. The following morning a wrecker came out from town, went up the mountain, and brought down the car. By mid-afternoon the party was on its way to California via a snowless route.

For forty-eight hours Painted Canyon Ranch had been a sort of International House with as interesting guests as we ever entertained. Both of us were particularly taken with the mother. Her matriarchal dignity was almost regal, and the disgust for the predicament her Swiss offspring had gotten them into was obvious. Several times she sat silent, staring at him fixedly. When a lull came in the conversation, she would announce in heavily accented deliberation: "My - son, - he - is - a - very - great - fool." She was greatly taken with Barney, and expressed her solemn opinion: "That cat should be in an ex - po - sis - ione."

On parting, the Zurich designer was profuse in his thanks for our hospitality and kissed Phyllis's hand with continental gallantry. After they had gone she said to me, "He admired my Mexican blouse, and asked me what size I wore. Do you suppose by any chance he means to send me one of his smart ski outfits?"

His token of gratitude arrived a month later from Switzerland. It was a pound box of very stale chocolates.

Visitors to southern Arizona sometimes lament the lack of a definite change in seasons. They miss the burgeoning life of spring and the brilliant fall colors of the eastern and northern states. This lack may be true in the lower desert areas but it doesn't apply to our sky island. There we had many springs and many autumns each year. Spring starts in the valleys around the first of April and reaches the mountaintops by early June; autumn begins its descent in October and arrives at the base around the middle of December. So for four months we could enjoy the delights of the changing seasons somewhere within a few miles.

We called on an arthritic lady from Ohio who was housebound in Tucson. It was October and she was nostalgic for her country home.

"Oh, if I could only see the hills splashed with autumn colors," she sighed.

Next week we returned. The back of the station wagon was filled with golden boughs of aspen, clusters of bright red maple leaves, and masses of russet oak foliage. We decorated the lady's room with them.

In general Phyllis and I are against raiding Nature. But when we saw the light of pleasure come into our friend's eyes, we felt justified in our vandalism this one time.

12 *The Three C's*

The so-called Three C's—Cows, Copper, and Climate—dominate the life and economy of Arizona's southeastern corner. They are the basis for the region's customs, outlook, and mores. Since the days of the Spaniards, more than two centuries ago, cattle and mine dumps have been a part of the scenery. Climate until recently was recognized only as a factor of the cattle business, rather than as an important independent resource. However, eventually it may prove to be the greatest of the Three C's.

The mining boom really began back in 1877 when Ed Schiefelin set out from the Indian-fighting army post of Fort Huachuca to prospect the barren, Apache-infested country east of the San Pedro River valley.

"All you'll find is your tombstone," the soldiers warned him.

But they were wrong. Ed struck one of the richest silver veins the world has ever known. He called his mine The Tombstone, and a lusty, rip-roaring camp with that lugubrious name suddenly sprang up in the desert hills. The population zoomed to seven thousand five hundred in three years. Its history is livelier than any fiction, and it topped the list of Western mining towns for downright vicious lawlessness. In Tombstone hell-raising became almost a civic duty. During its heyday in the 1880's, more bandits, gamblers, prostitutes, gunfighters, and desperadoes walked Tombstone's streets than any other place in the country, with the Earp-Clanton shooting fray at the O K Corral probably the most famous exchange of whistling lead in the West.

The camp had only a decade of active life until underground water flooded the mines. But Tombstone possessed too rugged a constitution to become a ghost. And it didn't—quite. In recent years the community has been restored as an Old Wild West museum piece, which attracts thousands of tourists, while loyal Tombstonians have ambitions to make their unique town a health resort and retirement center, boasting that they have the finest year-round climate in the United States. The staid and conservative Weather Bureau tends to go along with them on this.

However, there are ghosts aplenty in the hills and canyons of southeastern Arizona. Throughout the region are the crumbling adobe skeletons of once husky mining camps, each with its stirring sagas relating the brave deeds of the boom days. Some maintain a sleepy suspended animation, serving as post offices and general stores for surrounding ranches while waiting to be reborn. Miners' hopes never die.

The Chiricahua Mountains have their share of ghost towns. Galeyville and Paradise are a couple of former mining camps in Turkey Creek Canyon on the east slope, four to five miles north of Painted Canyon Ranch. Galeyville is far older and occupies a small but notorious niche in Arizona history. During the town's short life its bad men were badder and good citizens fewer than anywhere else in the Territory. One chronicler called Galeyville "the worst town in Arizona, perhaps the worst in the West." The reason was that the remote situation made the place a secure hide-out for rustlers, horse thieves, hijackers, and murderers. When things got too hot for lawbreakers in Tombstone, they headed for the Chiricahuas. Even the Cochise County sheriff learned that collecting taxes in Galeyville was neither healthy nor profitable.

The town was named after John H. Galey who came to Tombstone in 1879. He had made a fortune in pioneer Pennsylvania oil wells, but was bitten by the Western mining bug. Hearing of a silver strike in Turkey Creek Canyon, Galey prospected the area and located the Texas Mine, which looked good. Lured by the New Eldorado, others followed and Galeyville was laid out in 1880, mushrooming into a community of four hundred souls within a few months. Most of the structures were wood and canvas, but there were six general stores and ten saloons. A weekly newspaper expired with the third issue. A one-time resident later reminisced that "every five minutes or so day and night, somebody seemed to be firing a gun, and the doctors had a fine practice patching people together." It is also recorded that the frequenters of the dance

Gleeson, near "ghost" mining town.

hall "used to shoot the French heels off the slippers of the girls whirling in the quadrille."

Galeyville died in 1883 as suddenly as it had been born. John Galey's mine turned out to be nothing but a hole in the ground into which he had poured one hundred and eighty thousand dollars. He departed for the East leaving more creditors than friends. But he borrowed money, returned to Arizona, and honorably paid his mining debts. Later he recouped his fortune in Texas oil and died in 1918, full of years and a highly respected citizen of Beaver, Pennsylvania.

Phyllis and I, of course, inspected the site of Galeyville and found nothing but the suggestion of a stone wall, said to be the remains of the jail. This seems doubtful because law enforcement was a neglected activity. There was never anybody in Galeyville capable of arresting anyone else. Today the site is a grassy mesa scattered with oaks where cattle peacefully graze. It's difficult to visualize the explosive camp seething with trigger-happy adult delinquents. However, recently new life has come to Galeyville; lots are being sold and plans are afoot to create a Western frontier community complete with all modern conveniences.

Like most historians everywhere, the chroniclers of Arizona's past seldom agree on details. This applies to the naming of Paradise, the second Chiricahua mining town a way up Turkey Creek from Galeyville. I like the version which relates that the patriarch of our Painted Canyon Ranch, Stephan Reed, had a daughter who married an ambitious young man named George A. Walker. Around the turn of the century the newlyweds moved to a tree-shaded spot along Turkey Creek and, because of their happiness, christened it Paradise. I prefer this to hot and weary ore teamsters resting and watering their horses at a stream crossing they likened to heaven. Somehow that isn't in character.

George Walker was a miner who had a good thing in silver going for him among the nearby hills. So good that in 1901 a company was formed, and close to a half million dollars were spent in development work. Almost overnight Paradise became a town with a couple of big stores, thirteen saloons, and a two-story hotel. But the mines shut down in 1907 and Paradise today consists of a few weatherbeaten frame buildings and gaping foundations along a narrow, winding mountain road.

Several sporadically active southeastern Arizona mines still furnish some gold, silver, and other valuable metals. But it was the growth of the giant copper industry that changed mining from a pioneer, individualistic, hit-or-miss enterprise into big business on an international scale. Arizona is the country's leading copper state, and Bisbee mines have produced nearly a billion dollars worth. Bisbee ores are processed at the big Phelps Dodge smelter at Douglas, and the prosperity of the entire area goes up or down with the price of copper on the world market. Of the Three C's, Copper is the most important today.

Jesuit missionary explorer, Father Kino, introduced cattle into this then wild and barbarous northern border of New Spain around 1690. He was Arizona's first cowman. His prosperous Indian missions maintained herds numbering several thousand. Then, after the Gadsden Purchase of 1854 transferred the region from Mexico to the United States, Yankee settlers brought in Texas longhorns and other tough breeds to graze the grassy open ranges of the Public Domain. But cow punching was a hazardous occupation until the Apaches were vanquished in 1886. That epochal event triggered cattle raising as southeastern Arizona's chief economic activity. Although no longer so, it is still the predominant influence that shapes the peoples' thinking, activities, and way of life. Nowhere else in the world are there so many automobile bumper stickers reading "Eat Beef—Keep Slim."

In 1888 the San Simon Cattle Company took over thousands of acres by force in the valley east of the Chiricahuas. At one time the outfit ran fifteen thousand head of cattle and shipped as many as eight-thousand a year east by the new railroad. Although the company hadn't a shred of title to the land, all squatters were summarily evicted from the area. "They paid the willing ones in silver and the stand-patters with lead," said a contemporary commentator. In those times rival cattlemen waged continuous warfare for water-holes and the best grass. Lawlessness, violence, and sudden death were an integral part of raising beef on the hoof.

Brahmas, particularly suited to southern Arizona's arid ranges.

Some order began to emerge from the sea of chaos in the 1890's. The federal government's lands were classified and Arizona Territory enacted laws regarding water rights. Among the many Acts aimed at protecting Western resources none has had more far-reaching effects than the Bill passed by Congress in 1891 which conferred upon the President power to establish Forest Reserves. Chiricahua Forest Reserve was created by Theodore Roosevelt in 1902, later becoming Chiricahua National Forest, then the Chiricahua Division of Coronado National Forest. In 1906 established grazing rights were officially recognized on specified areas in the National Forests and other lands, both state and federal.

So today, southeastern Arizona cattle ranches usually consist of a core of deeded private holdings, surrounded by thousands of acres of publicly owned land leased for grazing. On the Flying H Phyllis and I held outright only about four hundred acres—the rest was Forest Service allotment. Although grazing leases are legally good for one year only and are renewed annually, actually they are as much a part of a ranch as is the deeded land. Allotments are bought, sold, and inherited along with the private property and are seldom changed or cancelled. This gives the rancher the feeling of ownership. However, each year he must sit down with the district Forest Service ranger or other official, and together they go over the grazing situation. Almost always the ranger wants to cut the number of cattle; the rancher strives to raise the ante. Like a poker game, the play goes on for some time until a reasonably satisfactory compromise is reached. Rancher and ranger then shake hands and the former has a grazing permit for another year.

This system has worked well for half a century. But beneath the surface stockmen resent being told what to do with their "property," particularly by outsiders, newcomers, or government men. In fact, the Arizona Cattle Growers Association passes a solemn resolution at its annual convention calling for all federal land to be turned over to the state. Phoenix is much easier managed by the cattle lobby than Washington.

In some places the differences of opinion have broken out in active antagonism. But mostly the two sides work out their problems amicably and take it out in sly digs at each other. Several years ago Pete Kinney, a grizzled stockman who had a ranch in San Simon Valley was asked to introduce the new Chiricahua District Ranger at a range management meeting. He got to his feet and addressed the gathering: "I am reminded of the time the Bible says the devil took our Savior to the top of an exceeding high mountain and showed him the kingdoms of the world spread out below. 'All these things I will give thee, if thou wilt fall down and worship me,' said Satan. And, do you know, the son-of-a-gun didn't own an acre of it. I would like to introduce Ranger Jones."

The Chiricahua Mountains are divided into a dozen or so Forest Service cattle allotments. The Coronado National Forest land surrounding the Painted Canyon Ranch is leased to a Portal rancher for grazing a small herd of Herefords. Our place was completely fenced, but open gates, downed wires, and bovine persistence made our water and lush grass easily available most of the time. Driving unwelcome cows off the premises was one of our regular ranch chores. Cattle aren't legally trespassers in Arizona, and if a landowner doesn't want to be overrun by his neighbor's cattle, it's up to him to keep them out. The stockman has no responsibility in the matter. On this one-sided basis we did the best we could, but it was seldom good enough.

One afternoon I was hot, tired, and much in need of a shower. But when I turned on the water in the bathroom, brown, muddy needles of liquid sprayed from the shower head.

"Oh! Oh!" I said and redressed in a hurry:

Len Banks and I went over to the main spring. It is cement-walled, about seven feet deep, and usually more than half filled. Heavy boards are laid across the top. But not this time! A cow had broken through the boards and fallen into the spring. She wasn't hurt and stood quiet and patient, half immersed in opaque, roiled-up water. Len got the block-and-tackle, and by attaching one end of the rope around the cow's horns and using the boards as a ramp, we got her out by dark. She objected strenuously to such discourteous treatment, and we ended wet as frogmen. After this incident we fenced the spring. Thereafter it was known as Geronimo's Stockade.

Another thing Phyllis and I learned about the cattle business at the Flying H. It's embarrassing, if not downright impertinent, to ask a rancher how many head he runs. That's similar to inquiring about his bank balance. This was invariably the first question our friends put to us at the Flying H, and we would answer vaguely, "Oh, quite a few." Then sometimes I parried the query by saying that I wore the biggest Stetson and had the smallest herd of any rancher at Harold Thurber's annual cattle sale and barbecue. Among cattle people there are no pretentions or ostentation. I never met one who was projecting an "image" or had any use for status symbols. Some of the region's most prosperous ranchers drive low-priced cars, live modestly, and are barely distinguishable from their less affluent neighbors.

The third C—Climate—is all important. Good feed is the foundation of the cattle business, and generous rains are essential to its prosperity. In fact, water is the life blood of the region, and the throbbing pump is the beating heart of every ranch. However, there has never been quite enough moisture to go around; water is always southeastern Arizona's greatest concern. Each winter storm and summer shower is watched as anxiously as stock market operators scan the ticker tape. "Getting mighty dry," is a standard conversational gambit. It is told that when Noah looked out of the Ark on the forty-first morning of The Flood and announced that the weather was clearing, an Arizona cowboy aboard remarked, "Yeah, but what we need is one more good rain."

Arizona rains are spotty and capricious; each rancher believes that he is skipped while adjacent ranges get the downpours. Big Dan Ming, prominent old-time politician and stockman of Sulphur Spring Valley, put this feeling into words in a prayer opening a cattlemen's meeting at Willcox. It was an extremely dry year. "Oh Lord," he said, "I am about to round you up for a good plain talk. Now Lord, I ain't like these fellows who come bothering you every day. This is the first time I ever tackled you for anything, and if you will only grant this, I'll promise never to bother you again. We want rain, good Lord, and we want it bad, and we ask you to send us some. But if you can't or don't want to send us any, for Christ's sake don't make it rain up around Hooker's or Veitch's ranges, but treat us all alike. Amen."

The old days of pioneer Arizona are over. The geographically isolated southeastern corner is perhaps the last to show the change, but a quiet revolution is going on there. The region is being rediscovered by a new generation of pioneers who are making the country into something very different from what it was. These new people are Chicago businessmen, Iowa farmers, retired Ohioans, ex-army officers, writers, artists, and health seekers from almost everywhere. Some of them have considerable means, most of them enjoy leisure, and all feel that they have found an agreeable and stimulating environment. More than anything else, it is the Climate that pleases them most.

People like the various brands of weather on tap in southeastern Arizona for many reasons—some of these being distinctly odd. There was, for example, The Case Of The Desiccated Scandinavian. The first episode occurred on a trip Phyllis and I made to California in late May. We spent a couple of days at Yosemite Valley, and I took the path into the ravine at the foot of Yosemite Falls. At the end, close to the roaring deluge, sat a fully clothed man drenched with spray and bathed in mist. We couldn't talk there by the thundering waters, but he came out with me and told his strange tale as he stood dripping in the warm sunshine.

"I'm a Norwegian," he said. "My home is now Southern California. I like it but can't stand the long dry season—month after month without a drop of moisture. It nearly drives me crazy."

"Well, this ought to fix you up," I said.

"Oh no. You don't understand. It isn't the same thing at all. I've got to see rain, feel rain, and smell rain." He thumped his chest dramatically. "I'm dried out through to my bones."

"Why don't you try Arizona?" I asked him.

"Arizona! That's desert—drier then it is here."

"Not in the summer," I said. But he wasn't convinced.

We exchanged cards and went our ways. "I'm going to try the Pacific Northwest next," were his parting words.

Back at the ranch toward the end of June the puffy little clouds that had been playing around the Chiricahuas for a week or so got together and built up into towering white thunderheads. After a long, parched spring, we got out first welcome rains. Then every

112

afternoon for two weeks showers crisscrossed the country every-where. It wasn't long before the papers began to carry stories of cloudbursts, floods, washed-out bridges, and blocked highways. Our rainy season had gotten out of hand, as it sometimes does.

One July day after lunch, as distant thunder growled on the di-vide, a car drove up to the gate. It had a California license, and I recognized the man who got out. It was my Norwegian Yosemite friend. We welcomed him, sat him down, and put on the coffee pot.

"How was your trip to the Northwest?" we asked him.

"Dry!" he said disgustedly.

"And Arizona?"

"Wonderful! On the way over it rained so hard twice I couldn't see to drive and had to stop; a flash flood held me up for three hours; and once I drowned my motor and was towed ten miles." His eyes sparkled. "Never felt better in my life!"

As I went to the kitchen for a second round of coffee and Phyllis scurried around for some solid refreshments, it began to sprinkle, and in a matter of minutes the heavens let loose with a deafening downpour. Water cascaded off the roof, the dry stream-bed beside the house was quickly transformed into a swift-running torrent, and the curtains of rain cut visibility to near zero.

When we returned the living room was empty. Our guest had vanished although his car was still in the drive. Then we looked out the back window. There in a puddle stood the desiccated Norwe-gian. Water poured from him in rivulets, and his face was lifted to the driving rain, eyes closed, with a look of sheer ecstasy.

13 *The Climate Ladder*

The mountain road from Rodeo over the Chiricahua divide at Onion Saddle and down the west side into Sulphur Spring Valley is about thirty-five miles long. It is narrow, winding, and steep in places, but can be made in less than two hours. A dead-end spur leads south from the Saddle skirting the crest for three miles to Rustler Park at an elevation of 8,400 feet. There a four-mile foot- and horse-trail climbs to the fire tower on Flys Peak, 1,250 feet higher. The lookout's little glass-enclosed room is more than 5,600 feet above Rodeo. The changes in climate and vegetation on a trip from base to summit are so rapid that one has the feeling of riding a rocket northward at 1,000 miles an hour.

In the Southwest temperatures drop sharply with increasing altitude. The lapse rate is generally about 1 degree F. for every 300 feet, which is roughly equivalent to a north-south difference of 300 miles for each 1,000 feet gain in elevation. This puts the top of Flys Peak climatically about 1,680 miles north of Rodeo. Mountains are also everywhere producers of moisture, and precipitation on their slopes usually increases with elevation. Thus Rodeo, in the San Simon Valley, has an annual average precipitation of 11 inches; Portal, 600 feet higher, registers more than 18 inches; while at Painted Canyon Ranch one year we collected over 26 inches of rain and melted snow in our measuring gauge. No weather stations exist in the high country, but annual precipitation there undoubtedly averages thirty-five inches, and in some spots probably more.

About seventy years ago naturalist C. Hart Merriam studied the biology of the isolated San Francisco Peaks in northern Arizona. He concluded that differences in climate, vegetation, animal, and bird life due to elevation closely matched those due to latitude.

From his observations he worked out a system of altitudinal "Life Zones" which band the mountains like layers in a pousse café. Each zone is based on a characteristic combination of temperatures and precipitation which results in similar life communities wherever found. For example, the spruce-fir-aspen association above 9,000 feet in the Chiricahua Mountains is found at ever-lower altitudes to the north until it reaches sea level in central Canada. This is called the Hudsonian Zone because its ecology resembles that around the southern shores of Hudson Bay. Topping it in Merriam's system is the Arctic-Alpine Zone above timberline, with climate and plant growth similar to the cold, barren lands of the Far North. In Arizona, the San Francisco Peaks are the only mountains high enough to reach up into this zone. Below the Hudsonian, in descending order, are the Canadian, Transition, Upper Sonoran, Lower Sonoran, and Tropical zones.

Altogether these seven life communities represent a biotic cross-section of western North America from Bering Sea to southern Mexico and, with alterations and adjustments, they were subsequently extended to include the entire continent. Merriam's arrangement has weaknesses, and is now seldom used by biologists and ecologists, who have substituted for it the more comprehensive biome concept. Biomes are based on major landscape units, such as grasslands, savannas, deciduous and coniferous forests, tundras, deserts, and so on, with a broad blend zone, or ecotone, between each major region. However, for the layman, the life-zone classification is the most graphic and dramatic way of demonstrating the amazing biotic differences in small, concentrated areas, such as the steep mountain slopes of southeastern Arizona's sky islands. There, five of the seven North American life zones are stacked one above another within a few miles—only the Arctic-Alpine and Tropical zones are missing.

An article of mine on the subject, called "Climbing the Climate Ladder," interested an Illinois newspaper editor. He wrote: "If I come out, will you take me on the kind of trip you describe?"

I answered, "Yes."

The editor and his wife arrived one afternoon in early June, and we made our climatic escalade the next morning. To include the

Hudsonian forest of spruce and aspen near the top of Flys Peak.

lowest rung of the ladder, we first drove down to Rodeo as a starting point. It was a bright, sunny day comfortable for shorts and light shirts. When we pointed the car back toward the Chiricahuas, the time was 9:15 A.M., and the temperature reading was 82 degrees F. on the maximum-minimum recording thermometer we hung in the shade of a gnarled, old mesquite tree, just out of town.

June is the warmest month of the year in southeastern Arizona, because it lacks the cooling effect of the clouds and showers that come in July and August.

A sparse growth of yucca, cactus, ocotillo, creosote bush, and other stunted desert shrubs characterize the valley floor around Rodeo as the Lower Sonoran. This is the hottest and driest life zone in the Southwest and extends from sea level to about 4,000 feet. It is named after the Mexican State of Sonora where such arid conditions are common. As we approached the mountains, desert vegetation gave way to expanses of grassland, indicating we were entering the next higher zone, the Upper Sonoran, which goes to an elevation of around 6,500 feet. Ahead the gold-brown grassy foothills and lower mountain slopes, not yet greened by the summer rains, were dotted with oaks which increased with altitude to streaks and patches of woodland. Although called "evergreen," the Emory, Arizona white, and Mexican blue oaks of the Upper Sonoran Zone are not quite so. They have the strange habit of carrying their foliage through the winter, then turning color, shedding, and putting out new leaves in the spring, all within a month. Visitors at this season are apt to think that our bare oaks are dead.

Life zones are not separated by sharp lines of demarcation. The kinds of plants in any one place depend upon slope exposure, type of soil, ground moisture, and microclimatic differences, as well as altitude. So there is a good deal of inter-fingering of species upward and downward from their typical habitat, and in some cases pockets of one zone are found within another. An example of major zone displacement occurs in Cave Creek Canyon just above Portal. Because of a permanently high water table and cold air drainage from the elevated rim of the large interior basin beyond, species from the cooler, more humid Transition Zone descend and mingle with Upper Sonoran vegetation on the floor of the canyon. As we followed the course of the creek I pointed out to the Editor the first Chihuahua pines, Apache pines, Arizona cypress, deciduous oaks, ashes, and maples. These are all, strictly speaking, Transition Zone trees.

We stopped at Painted Canyon Ranch and partook of a second breakfast on the veranda with the ladies. The temperature was in the middle seventies, and the air was fresh with the scent of growing things and a faint aroma of lilac from the blossoming bushes by the front steps. With an altitude of 5,340 feet, the ranch is basically in the Upper Sonoran Zone, but the ecologies, like those in the canyon below, are somewhat scrambled. I never made a serious study of the vegetation, but counted more than fifty species of woody perennial plants typical of the Lower Sonoran, Upper Sonoran, and Transition zones within a half mile of the house. I'm not botanist enough to know all the wildflowers that bloomed in our meadows and woods from April to October. But by the book I identified blossoms representative of four out of the five life zones.

The south-facing slope across the road rises without a break 2,600 feet up to the pink cliffs crowning Silver Peak like a huge helmet. It is mostly steep-pitched open grassland with a scattering of Upper Sonoran oaks, alligator junipers, and spiky, orange-flowered agaves, but some of the smaller shrubs are desert species. The main stream and branch beside the house are bordered by fine groups of sycamores, walnuts, willows, and cottonwoods, some of the last being grand arching specimens, more than seventy feet tall. In addition there are a few imported trees, such as the graceful weeping willow by the spring on the front lawn and the row of arrowy Lombardy poplars behind the swimming pool. I also planted several Mediterranean Aleppo pines and Himalayan deodars which apparently liked out climate. Across Cave Creek a mesa rises gently southward for a half-mile, covered with an unbroken woodland of oaks and Chihuahua pines. A shallow ravine which breaks the mesa's surface harbors Arizona cypress and a few Douglas firs, a tree more at home in the Canadian Zone, 2,000 feet above.

One of the principal reasons for these anomalies in the distri-

The creamy blossoms of yucca in June.

bution of plants and animals on steep mountain slopes is the slow change in climate through the centuries. This can result in shifting the zone elevations vertically hundreds of feet up or down. Experts, who know about such things, say that during the Pleistocene Epoch, twenty to twenty-five thousand years ago, the Hudsonian Zone was about 4,000 feet lower than it is today, and precipitation was considerably greater. At that time timberline in the Chiricahuas must have been around 8,000 feet, and ponderosa pines then grew in the valleys. This was in the last glacial period when vast sheets of ice buried the northern part of the continent. Vegetation was forced southward, and it was then that the coniferous forest migrated to the Southwest and became established there.

With a world-wide warming trend, the glaciers retreated and plant life followed the waning ice northward. But on the island-like mountain ranges of southeastern Arizona there was another direction available to the cold-climate vegetation—straight up. So the life zones climbed to higher and higher elevations. As the weather continued to moderate, the Arctic-Alpine was snuffed out on the mountaintops, and the Hudsonian was also extinguished except for two widely separated patches on the summits of the Chiricahuas and Pinalenos. About ten thousand years ago condi-

The ranch is basically Upper Sonoran but ecologies are mixed.

The cliffs of Silver Peak above the meadow,
Upper Sonoran and desert species.

tions were right for an invasion of Mexican highland grasslands and oak-juniper woodlands with their accompanying fauna. These pre-empted the valleys and lower mountain slopes abandoned by the conifers. They are still there. The pinyon of the Chiricahuas is also the Mexican species. The ubiquitous pinyon-juniper association to the north is lacking, apparently having been blocked by intervening desert areas.

Most animals and many birds went upward with their congenial life zones and became marooned in small enclaves on the slopes of the various ranges. Some with common ancestors have lived apart long enough to differentiate into distinct species. Thus, the Chiricahua Mountains are inhabited by the Apache squirrel; the Hua-chuca Mountains have a different species, the Huachuca gray squirrel; and localized varieties of the latter appear in other sky islands.

Since the close of the last glacial period there have been several minor fluctuations when the climate was cooler and more moist or warmer and drier than today. With each change the life zones have moved up or down. In every case local conditions have enabled some vegetation to persist at altitudes no longer best suited to it. That is, plants typical of any zone may be found above or below their present optimum elevation. The most striking example of such a relict life community is on the Snowshed Trail a mile or so from Painted Canyon Ranch. There, on a south-facing slope, is a stand of the oldest and largest ocotillos I have ever seen. This plant, which resembles a bundle of thorny coach whips growing from a common stem, is an indicator of the desert Lower Sonoran Zone. Across the canyon the mountainside is covered with a Transition forest of cypress and ponderosa pine. These ocotillos are 2,000 feet above their present normal range, which suggests that there was a time, perhaps several hundred years ago, when temperatures averaged five to six degrees higher than now. But if so, one wonders why the tenuous Hudsonian Zone wasn't exterminated at the summit of the range.

The Editor and I could easily have spent another leisurely hour on the porch. But duty called. We had a climate ladder to scale. So we reluctantly left the ladies, donned slacks, and packed jackets and a couple of box lunches in a knapsack. We then took off on the next leg of our journey.

Beyond Painted Canyon Ranch we started our winding ascent to the lofty backbone of the Chiricahuas. The road slanted upwards, curving in and out across the ribs of the mountains. Each succeeding corner gave us ever-widening views down into the rock-walled green bowl of Cave Creek basin and out over the level amber stretches of San Simon Valley, past barren, wrinkled hills to distant New Mexican mountains lining the eastern horizon.

On the final steep pull to Onion Saddle an increasingly heavy growth of ponderosa pines and deciduous oaks announced that we

Rustler Park, Transition Zone.

A stream is born high in an Englemann spruce forest.

Atop Flys Peak, the Canadian Zone.

had left the Upper Sonoran and set foot on the next higher rung of the ladder, the Transition. At 11:45 A.M. the Editor and I reached the road-end at Rustler Park, left the car, and started up the trail to Flys Peak on foot. The temperature was 66 degrees F. and we donned our jackets for the climb. This was the Canadian Zone, with a climate resembling northern Maine or Wisconsin.

We trudged upwards through cool, shady forests of white fir, Douglas fir, and Mexican white pines; traversed needle-spiced open stands of stately cinnamon-boled ponderosas; passed fern-banked streams; and crossed meadows amidst early blooming gardens of wild iris. The last mile of trail up the rounded dome of Flys Peak threaded a somber forest of Engelmann spruce interspersed with groves of aspen decked in quaking leaves of new spring green.

The Editor was impressed. "This isn't southern Arizona," he exclaimed several times. "It's the North Woods!"

It was breezy on top and fluffy white pre-monsoon clouds scuttled across the blue sky not far above our heads. When they blotted out the sun the 62-degree temperature felt chilly. But the Editor and I picked a sheltered spot among the summit rocks. There we had lunch and looked back down the climate ladder we had ascended from the shining valley more than a vertical mile below.

The maximum reading on our thermometer at Rodeo that day was 102 degrees.

14 High Country

Whenever time and opportunity allowed, I took off with a light pack to explore our backdoor mountains. So in numerous one- to three-day trips afoot, on trail and off, I covered some five hundred miles among the hidden, high-pocket valleys, airy ridges and summits of the divide. I camped in deep woods and watched the setting sun gild the tips of spire-like firs as hermit thrushes sang their evening song; spread my bed atop 9,796-foot Chiricahua Peak under a full moon with the twinkling lights of the distant valley far below; built campfires beside bubbling springs and murmuring streams; and snowshoed through the silent white winter forests. Yet on none of these wanderings was I more than a few hours' walk from home.

I have never known friendlier or more appealing high country. There are trails reaching every part of the range, and I have traveled nearly all of them. Chief artery is the Crest Trail which starts near Rustler Park and ambles casually southward for twelve miles along the broad backbone of the Chiricahuas. This delectable skyline pathway seldom drops below an elevation of 9,000 feet, and it tunnels superb stands of evergreens and groves of white-stemmed aspens, crosses verdant natural parks, and comes out on rocky points overlooking thousands of square miles of mountains, valleys, mesas and plateaus. The main trail is joined by laterals on both east and west sides, and has extensions that follow ridges and canyons to road-ends in the southern part of the range.

The going is easy on the Chiricahuas' exhilarating, unspoiled rooftop, and the dome-like summits, rounded ridges, and meadowed glades invite leisurely off-trail investigation. For, surprisingly enough, these rugged mountains culminate in a high-perched area of subdued contours and gentle relief, measuring about six miles from north to south and more than a mile wide.

Whenever time allowed, I took off with a light pack.

The only logical explanation seems to be that the present summit topography represents a row of former lowland hills lifted bodily by block-faulting five thousand feet into the air, where they have remained little changed for several million years. The same geological phenomenon is evident in many southwestern mountain ranges.

Along the Crest Trail are several Forest Service log cabins used for administratvie purposes. They are delightfully situated on top of the peaks or nestled in green, wooded glades. Although I had my favorite camping spots, these snug refuges were hard to forego. As a temporary employee on summer fire duty and snow observer in winter, I carried keys that were the open sesame to the comfort of warm blankets and the luxuries of stoves, cots, tables, chairs, and gasoline lamps. There, too, were the smell of woodsmoke, the patter of rain on the roof, the roar of the wind outside, and the muffled blur of falling snow through the windows. To me, log cabins are a nostalgic heritage from America's past. They embody the traditional pioneer spirit of those who left civilization and pushed forward into the primitive wilderness.

The Chiricahua cabins were built by the C.C.C. under the direction of Fred Winn, Coronado National Forest Supervisor from 1926 to 1943. He was before my time, and I never met him, but he left a memory that has become almost a legend. Cosmopolite and artist, Fred Winn was equally at home at a Paris sidewalk café or playing poker in an Arizona cow camp. When a curious friend asked him why he gave up art for the Forest Service, he answered: "I got tired of painting nude women." The 365-foot Sally Falls, which we could see from the ranch, were recently renamed Winn Falls in his honor.

However, I was barely tolerated as a guest by the permanent cabin residents. Each is in complete possession of a family of white-footed deer mice whose feverish nocturnal activities continue full-tilt in spite of human invasion. One night at Cima Park Guard Station a tinny rattle, far noisier and more insistent than routine mouse business, got me up to inspect. My flashlight revealed a flip-lidded ash tray hopping about the table. With a paternal, "Let that be a lesson to you," I went back to sleep, intending to release the diminutive prisoner in the morning. But during the night the super-mouse pushed the tight-fitting top off the ash tray and escaped.

Another time at the lofty Flys Peak Lookout Cabin I was awakened by violent splashing. A mouse had fallen into the water pail and was swimming around frantically trying to find dry land. I poured him on the ground outside, but five minutes later he was back in the cabin endeavoring to open a package of brown sugar. Besides these lively occupants, raccoons, foxes, porcupines, skunks, deer, and other four-footed callers drop by and keep a cabin visitor from having any sense of loneliness; both day and night one is impressed by the busy, teeming life that goes on in this sky island high above the southern Arizona desert.

I don't subscribe to the generally accepted idea that animals possess keener senses than humans. It seems to me that quite the reverse is true. Over and over again I have spotted animals or birds and watched them conduct their private affairs while no miraculous built-in radar warned them that a human Peeping Tom was in the vicinity. Members of the cat tribe are an exception. I have occasionally caught sight of the tawny, fleeting flash of a retreating wildcat, but he apparently always saw me first. Nor have I ever surprised a cougar, although I have seen their tracks in both mud and snow.

The secret of seeing wildlife, of course, is being alone, unarmed, and on foot. Two people advertise their presence by conversation and large parties have little chance of observing the shyer creatures. But it's my experience that guns and trail scooters are the human inventions most feared, and they send game to cover for miles around.

Cima Park Guard Station, built by the C. C. C.

However, not all Chiricahua animals and birds are aloof and exclusive. Mexican chickadees and Arizona juncos are likely to follow one in the tree branches above, chirping the latest mountaintop news, and the pine woods often resound with the raucous calls of inquisitive long-crested blue jays. Some of the birds are natural show-offs and seem to enjoy performing before a human audience. This is particularly true of hummingbirds. Besides the half-dozen resident species at least nine more breed in the Chiricahuas.

I had a reserved grandstand seat for hummingbird shows on a dizzy point above a jutting cliff at the crest of the range. Four thousand feet below was the basin of Cave Creek with Painted Canyon Ranch a minute green spot on its floor. Usually when I arrived not a performer was in sight, but soon the air would be filled with fifteen to twenty darting hummingbirds. They whizzed around the cliff, chased each other, swooped by my head like miniature jet planes, and dropped in whistling, vertical dives, seventy-five to a hundred feet. There must be thousands of hummingbirds in the Chiricahuas, and I've seen several hundred of them swarm over the wild iris in Rustler Park with the sound of wingbeats resembling the drone of a distant bomber.

Wherever hummingbirds gather there are wildflowers, and these mountains spread an unsurpassed nectar banquet for them. Sunny slopes are brilliant with golden helenium, violet verbena, blue lupine, and crimson groundwort; meadows bloom with iris, composites, and larkspur six to seven feet high; while shady woods and moist stream banks are brightened by columbine, shooting stars, cardinal flowers, Indian paintbrush, silene, penstemon, mertensia, and scores of other varieties. Fourteen species of ferns have been found, and brakes of almost tropical luxuriance grow in the shelter of aspen groves and cover the slopes under the pines with a rich green carpet.

Then there are birds who live in the high rocky places. I know a remote pool on a Chiricahua stream up toward the crest where one can see a half-dozen eagles come to drink each evening. One summer day at sunset I was treated to a spectacular aerial show that surpassed even that of the hummingbirds. It was performed by violet-green swallows and white-throated swifts around the pointed top

*Four thousand feet below "Hummingbird Point" Painted Canyon Ranch
was a minute speck.*

Abandoned fire lookout, Silver Peak.

of Silver Peak. This isolated 7,975-foot mountain rises above Cave Creek Canyon well to the east of the divide. On the summit is an abandoned fire lookout station with cot and enough LP gas left in the stove to cook a few meals. On my last visit I sat outside on the rocks after supper and marveled at the careening, rocketing aeronautics of the darting swallows and swifts below, above, and around me until darkness drove us all to bed. The birds' antics appeared to be exuberant play after a serious day's work, and they seemed to enjoy having me as a spectator.

But perhaps my favorite feathered native Chiricahuan is the Merriam turkey. In summer the high parks and sun-warmed south-facing piney slopes are popular haunts of these big birds, and I like to look in on their family life unobserved as the hens feed, gossip, and dust themselves, while the males strut importantly back and forth as if on parade. Their "gobble-gobble" is similar to that of their domestic cousins. Although too heavy for level takeoff and actual flight, wild turkeys can sail onto tree branches from high slopes behind and roost there for the night. A thrilling sight is to see a flock of big toms, each weighing maybe twenty-five to thirty pounds, volplane down from a tall pine into the center of an open meadow.

South of Rustler Park is the Chiricahua Wilderness Area. Covering eighteen thousand acres, or about twenty-eight square miles, it preserves the highest part of the range intact in a wild, undisturbed condition. Established in 1931 during Fred Winn's administration, the area is now a unit of the nation-wide Wilderness Preservation System with assured protection guaranteed by the Wilderness Act passed by Congress in 1964. Roads and permanent buildings are taboo, and all motorized transport is prohibited. Travel is on foot or horseback only. Lumbering is also forbidden but, unlike the national parks, hunting and grazing are permitted in National Forest Wilderness Areas. A Los Angeles school teacher wrote me after a knapsack jaunt in the Chiricahuas: "It's really great to be able to get out to the peace and quiet of our wilderness areas—the country seems to be in a constant turmoil."

Fred Winn was a nature enthusiast and his foresight saved this unique mountaintop realm for the enjoyment, inspiration, and education of the more and more crowded generations to come. We are fortunate to possess such an easily accessible natural retreat. But some six square miles should be added to the southeast corner of the Wilderness Area to include the impressive, cliff-walled upper canyon of Cave Creek's South Fork. This slot-like gorge is one of the Chiricahuas' outstanding scenic features.

Rustler Park is a delightful small pine-rimmed meadow near the crest. During the 1880's it was a hideout for Galeyville horse and cattle thieves, who held stock there and in nearby Barfoot Park while they altered brands and waited for the hair to grow before selling the animals to valley ranchers. Such notorious outlaws as

Sam Bass, Sam Blue, and Billy the Kid are also said to have found asylum in this remote spot. Rustler Park is now a Forest Service Recreation Area, with developed camp sites and a summer ranger station. Another reminder of the past is Flys Peak, named for Camillas S. Fly, an early Tombstone photographer. He accompanied General George Crook on several Apache Indian campaigns and is particularly noted for his pictures of Geronimo.

Surrounding Rustler Park is the finest stand of ponderosa pines in the Chiricahua high country. Or perhaps I should say ponderosa-type pines. For in southern Arizona's sky islands this most widespread of Western conifers goes in for experimentation and diversity. It even discards the habit of being a three-needled tree and sports anywhere from two to seven needles in a bundle, sometimes all on the same tree. In the Chiricahuas, Huachucas, and

Rustler Park.

other mountains along the Mexican border, the ponderosa has a pair of close relatives which most dendrologists have separated into distinct species. They are the pompom-foliaged Apache pine and the five-needled Arizona pine. Then there is the more distantly related three-needled Chihuahua pine, which resembles an impoverished ponderosa with short needles and a host of small black cones. Still, one can find a few typical ponderosas among the profusion of variations.

No two trips to the high Chiricahuas were the same; each had surprises and revelations that are filed in my memory. But a few stand out with special prominence, such as the one in my mental card-index titled "Cloud Frost on the Heights."

This came in November when for three days the divide was hidden by churning, wind-blown clouds, and the temperature was well below freezing above 8,500 feet. No storm came, and not a drop of rain fell at Painted Canyon Ranch. Yet when the weather cleared, the forested upper slopes and ridges stood forth against the blue sky in dazzling white. Every rock and tree shone as if it had been silver plated, and not a dark blemish broke the gleaming surface anywhere.

Realizing this was something out of the ordinary, I drove up the road to Rustler Park and took the Crest Trail to have a look. Near the summit I entered a startling world of unreality which nearly took my breath away. Although there was no snow and the ground was bare, each pine, fir, and spruce along the divide was completely encased in ice. Trunks, branches, and even needles were outlined in white like the frosting on a cake, and delicate white "feathers" and pendants, from two to six inches long, trailed from every twig. Frozen mist blowing over the mountaintops had transformed the dark green forest into a fairyland that was almost blindingly brilliant. However, it was a temporary enchantment. The warm sun made short work of obliterating the chimeric caprice, and driving back down the mountain, I could hardly believe I had really seen it.

These knapsack jaunts of mine into our back-door high country were leisurely affairs, more akin to wandering than to hiking. Time schedules were forgotten, while routes and destinations were often left to chance—what seemed most interesting at the moment. It might be a secluded canyon I'd never looked into, a hidden stream where native trout lurked, or finding the southernmost stand of Engelmann spruce in the United States. I seldom wore a watch, never took a map, and usually departed from the ranch with a vague, "I'll be back tomorrow evening, or maybe the day after."

To me, knapsacking is one of the pleasantest ways yet invented to take a break from civilization. With a light pack on my back and a beckoning wilderness trail in front of me, I am on my own and free as a bird. I sometimes left home with several problems which had been bothering me, but up in the Chiricahua high country I couldn't seem to remember what they were. This is a rare and refreshing experience, like a voyage to outer space, but a lot safer. On a knapsack trip, too, each camp becomes home—a secure and sheltering haven that seems intimately your own. I have never made one I haven't hated to leave and look back upon some with

Each pine, fir, spruce was completely encased in ice.

considerable nostalgia. Etched in my memory is the spangled pine whose black branches against the night sky caught the stars like the myriad lights of a giant Christmas tree; the brilliant, crashing pyrotechnics of a nearby thunder storm from Sentinel Peak; or wind in the lofty treetops at Centella Point.

I am going back someday.

Much has been said and written about the importance of preserving a few remnants of America's rapidly dwindling original wilderness. No people ever fell heir to a more magnificent natural heritage. Saving some undisturbed open spaces, green spots, mountains, deserts, and ocean shores is becoming increasingly necessary for the revitalization of us computerized, electronically driven moderns. Renewed strength and mental energy pour into us from the wilderness, whether it be a few acres or thousands. Nerves re-

One of the pleasantest ways to take a break from civilization.

lax and pent-up emotions drain away. It is then that we can understand Tarzan in the jungle giving the wild, exuberant ape call and pounding his chest before swinging from tree to tree on handy lianas.

I have never sniffed glue, smoked marijuana or taken a "trip" with LSD. For "kicks" give me the wilderness. One night I sat on the tiptop of Monte Vista Peak in the Chiricahuas and looked down into the black void of Sulphur Spring Valley, a vertical mile below. There pinpoints of moving lights indicated lilliputian automobiles on the highway. Suddenly I was aware of a surge of irresistible power within me, and felt that I could descend the mountain and become the governor of Arizona. Nothing could stop me, and at the time it seemed an easy and logical thing to do. Next morning my political ambitions were gone, but the tingling exhilaration lingered. After scrambled eggs and bacon I decided to settle for being a world famous writer. So maybe we should include the wilderness in the category of psychedelic or mind-expanding drugs. My experience on Monte Vista Peak was similar to that of the LSD-user who jumped out of a fourth-story window because he thought he could fly.

But perhaps the greatest value in following these lofty skyland trails was the peace and satisfaction best found in Nature's unspoiled places. When the going gets tough down here below, I close my eyes and imagine myself on the crest of the Chiricahuas with the world at my feet.

No better tranquilizer was ever invented.

15 *Land of Standing Rocks*

If the Chiricahuas are perversely haunted by the Curse of Geronimo, they are also blessed by the wise and beneficent spirit of the
Apache chief, Cochise. The most celebrated and respected Indian
in southwestern history, Cochise is commemorated in many place
names of the region. There is Cochise County, which takes in the
entire southeastern corner of Arizona, a town called Cochise, and
Cochise Stronghold in the Dragoon Mountains west of Sulphur
Spring Valley. But the most prominent and lasting memorial to the
famous chief is Cochise Head which rises to an altitude of 8,109
feet in the northern part of the Chiricahuas. This colossal granite
profile with domed forehead, aquiline nose, and a hundred-foot
pine tree for an eyebrow, looks serenely up into the sky and is a fit-
ting monument to the former ruler of these wild mountains and
outspread valleys.

Below the huge stone face, on the western slope, is Chiricahua
National Monument. Familiarly known as The Wonderland Of
Rocks, it is twenty miles from Painted Canyon Ranch by way of the
little winding road that climbs over Onion Saddle and descends the
other side of the mountains. Phyllis and I proudly introduced the
Monument to our house guests as if it were our private preserve—
all except one lady from Massachusetts, who said, when we
suggested the usual personally conducted tour, "I don't like rocks."

Most of our friends were as taken with this weirdly beautiful
stone labyrinth as we were. Sometimes described as "Carlsbad
Caverns without a roof," our Wonderland is quite unlike any place
anywhere else. Geologists say that back in the Tertiary Period,
maybe fifteen million years ago, the ground shook, split open, and
spewed out flows of molten lava which covered the country to a
depth of several hundred feet. The lava cooled into solid rock and
was later slowly lifted up by the growing Chiricahua Mountains

Cochise Head looks serenely up into the sky.

and tilted toward the west. There today, from the crest almost to the base of the range, are the remains of the ancient volcanic field eroded through the centuries into a maze of fantastic rhyolite and basalt pinnacles, columns, spires, and balanced rocks. Sixteen square miles of the most spectacular formations were set aside as a National Monument by proclamation of President Coolidge in 1924.

Intimacy is one of the special charms of the area. It is like a small but perfect gem set among the enfolding green mountains. Deep amidst the towering rocks are secluded twisting canyons lined with oaks, pines, and cypresses. Beneath the trees decorous little streams drop from ledge to ledge in miniature cascades and waterfalls. We seldom walked in the Monument without finding flowers new to us and rare plants and birds we had never seen before. In fact, the place is a veritable outdoor museum of geology, botany, ornithology, and many other -ologies, with natural exhibits displayed as if in glass cases.

The introduction to the Wonderland is sudden and dramatic. The access road leaves broad, treeless Sulphur Spring Valley, to the west and enters a mountain canyon. Abruptly one is transported to another world. Desert cactus and yucca is replaced by oak and juniper woodlands, and ahead the high canyon walls bristle with myriads of gray-brown rock towers, needles, and obelisks.

The National Park Service Visitor Center is situated in a fine grove of oaks beside Rhyolite Creek at an elevation of 5,345 feet, and there are pleasant campgrounds and the Kents' guest ranch nearby. The seven-mile drive beyond to 6,850-foot Massai Point, on the Chiricahua crest, is an experience in sheer fantasy. The paved road ascends Bonita Canyon by easy grades, and on both sides rise huge stone toadstools, upended cigars, picket-topped cliffs, towers, pillars, and turrets. Among them are giant figures resembling people, animals, and objects, such as China Boy, with his square Oriental hat, the mitred Bishop, Praying Padre, the Boxing Glove, the Ugly Duckling, and the Cathedral. We never failed to find additions to the bizarre collection, and named a group of four upright rock figures the Beatles because their stone caps resemble mops of long hair. The canyon is thickly grown with Arizona cypress and in Bonita Park, above, the road passes several alligator junipers, more than six feet in diameter at the base. Their gray bark is checkered with small, square plates, looking somewhat like the thick, leathery skin of a saurian.

At Massai Point the trees thin out to stunted, windblown cypresses, pinyons, and junipers which have the picturesque outlines of Japanese prints. Here the road ends and short paths lead to outlooks over a wilderness of clustered stone monuments, canyons, and forests, and beyond to miles of valley grasslands sweeping away to distant mountains. The rugged, contorted chaos below is best explored afoot or on horseback over the fourteen miles of graded trails. Phyllis and I liked to wander the easy four-and-a-half-mile Echo Canyon Loop from Massai Point. It follows glens between stone battlements and pinnacles several hundred feet high,

A maze of fantastic columns and towers, with corridors barely wide enough to pass through.

then climbs through corridors among the soaring rocks barely wide enough to pass through in some places. Sequestered Echo Park, in the midst of the maze, is a delightful retreat shaded by oaks and tall ponderosa pines.

We often took our more ambitious guests on the longer eight-mile round trip to Heart of Rocks, an extensive array of outlandish figures, including Big Balanced Rock, Punch and Judy, Duck on a Rock, Queen Victoria, and hundreds more. Also a favorite stroll, particularly around sunset time, was the mile-long trail from Massai Point to the lookout house on Sugarloaf Mountain, 7,307 feet elevation.

This Land of Standing Rocks was an impregnable natural fortress of the Apaches, and one can well understand why no white man ventured within its hostile fastnesses. And even after the tribe was vanquished with the surrender of Geronimo in 1886, one lone survivor lived on here and held the world at bay. He was Bigfoot Massai, a wild and furtive savage who became almost a legend. For several years he fought off Americans, Mexicans, and tame reservation Indians. Kidnapping squaws, raiding ranches, stealing horses and cattle, Massai defied civilization. He was noted for his remarkably oversize feet, and his distinctive tracks were last seen in the Wonderland's Bonita Canyon around 1892. It is probable that he died somewhere among the huge standing rocks—proud, free, and unconquered.

Little is actually known about Massai, and many stories about him are pure inventions. Some say that he was deported to Florida with Geronimo's defeated band but escaped from the prison train and made his way back to the Chiricahuas; others, that he jumped the San Carlos Indian Reservation. At any rate, valley settlers had good reason to fear this untamed "bronco" Apache. One night Massai and a squaw raided Colonel Hughes Stafford's ranch. They broke mirrors and windows, smashed furniture, stole food, and made away with the Colonel's favorite horse. Stafford himself barely escaped with his life. The next day he took off after the red-skinned outlaws with a neighbor, ex-Sergeant Neil Erickson, a former army Indian fighter. Here again stories differ: they recovered the horse; found it three months later; it turned up at the

Colonel's ranch the following year. Take your pick. But whichever you choose, the pair never caught up with the elusive Indians.

The significance of this wild horse chase was that Stafford and Erickson were the first white men to see the startling formations of the Wonderland of Rocks. It was Erickson's daughter Lillian and her husband, Ed Riggs, who thoroughly explored the area and were instrumental in having it established as a National Monument. They discovered many of the scenic features and built the first trail. One time Ed Riggs took a party into the Wonderland to show them the Big Balanced Rock, which only he and his wife had seen. At a steep place along the way a woman in the group, named Sara Deming, slipped and tore a gaping hole in the seat of her pants. Aunt Martha Riggs, who always wore an apron in true pioneer style, quickly took it off and tied it around Miss Deming's waist backwards. The event is immortalized in the names Sara Deming Canyon and Sara Deming Trail.

Ed Riggs died in 1950. Phyllis and I never knew him. However, Lillian Riggs still lives at Faraway Ranch on the western edge of the Monument. We were always fascinated by her tales of bygone days, and amazed at her intimate knowledge of the Chiricahuas. Although Mrs. Riggs lost her eyesight some years ago, on a cross-mountain drive with her we found she could "see" as well as we could. She knew every turn, every view, and almost every tree. In fact, several times she told us to stop and look at something interesting we hadn't noticed before.

The Apaches called the high lookout in the Wonderland *Say Yahdesut*—Point of Rocks—and believed they could hear the voices of their dead whose spirits lingered there. Ed Riggs requested the Board on Geographic Names that it be officially christened Massai Point, after the last native inhabitant. I never encountered the fierce spirit of Massai on my frequent visits, but I harbor a certain empathy should such an encounter occur. We would agree that there are much worse places to live than Chiricahua National Monument. As American citizens Phyllis and I own about five square feet of it. But if the Lord of the Universe offered me a piece of original America to hold in fee simple, I'd choose the Land of Standing Rocks. There is more condensed scenery, wildlife and vegetation there than any other area of like size I know. We can't help feeling that the lady from Massachusetts who doesn't like rocks missed something special on her trip to Arizona.

After all, though, the biggest single feature of the panorama from Massai Point is Cochise Head, which dominates the skyline four miles to the northeast. This great profile rises as high above the point as the character of the chief did above the renegade Indian. For, savage and barbarous as he may have been, Cochise was one of the outstanding men in American history and ranks among the world's top generals as commander and strategist. He was mentally and physically superior to most of the Whites pitted against him, and it was the perfidy, cruelty and stupidity of so-called civilized men that changed him from a reliable ally into a vengeful enemy.

Up to 1860 Cochise was friendly with the white settlers. He believed that diplomacy was better for his people than warfare. On several occasions the chief prevented his tribesmen from molesting wagon trains and stagecoaches. But in October of that year a band of Pinal Apaches from the north raided a ranch, ran off the cattle

Wonderland of Rocks and Cochise Head.

and horses, and kidnapped the settler's stepson. The rancher appealed to the nearest army post, wrongly blaming Cochise and the Chiricahua Apaches for the outrage. The fort's commanding officer was short of mounted men at the time, and it wasn't until three months later that he dispatched a detail of twelve soldiers to recover the child. In charge was a recently graduated West Pointer, George N. Bascom.

There is nothing fundamentally wrong with second lieutenants. But when a green, inexperienced shavetail is sent out to do a colonel's job, anything can happen. Had a tactful and understanding older officer dealt with Cochise the subsequent history of Arizona might have been different.

Bascom and his men found the chief camped near the Butterfield Stage Station at Apache Pass in the extreme northern part of the Chiricahua Mountains. The Lieutenant invited Cochise and his braves to confer with him under the white flag of truce. When they assembled in the army tent, Bascom arrogantly demanded the return of the white boy and livestock. Cochise replied with quiet dignity that the Chiricahua Apaches were at peace with the Americans. For more than five years they had taken nothing belonging to the Whites. But he promised to send warriors to the other Apache tribes in an effort to have the boy and stock brought back. The discussion went on for an hour, then was abruptly terminated by Lieutenant Bascom.

"Cochise, you are a liar," he said. "You and your chiefs are my prisoners until the boy is returned."

With a good round English oath, Cochise jumped to his feet.

"I am no prisoner of yours!" he shouted. And from his breechclout he whipped out a knife, slashed the rear wall of the tent, and jumped through. Soldiers of the patrol fired at the fleeing chief, wounding him in the shoulder, but he zigzagged up the hill behind rocks and trees and disappeared, leaving a trail of blood. The other Indians were quickly subdued, one being knocked down by a gun butt and another stabbed with a bayonet. And still the white flag fluttered over Lieutenant Bascom's tent.

With rage in his heart, Cochise made for his stronghold in the Dragoons, thirty-five miles away. There he gathered a hundred warriors and returned to Apache Pass. Three white men were captured and offered in exchange for the imprisoned Indians. But Bascom ignored his countrymen's desperate pleas to be saved and once again demanded the return of the kidnapped boy. That was final. Infuriated, Cochise ordered that one of the white captives be tied behind his horse. Then, in full sight of Bascom and his soldiers, he put his horse to the gallop and dragged the man to his death over the sharp rocks. The other two were tortured and hung. In retaliation, Lieutenant Bascom hanged his Indian prisoners.

Thus began Cochise's war of vengeance against all white men. For the next eleven years hundreds of American travelers, settlers, and ranchers were shot, burned alive, or horribly tortured, and thousands of dollars worth of property was destroyed to pay for the mistake of one callow, young second lieutenant.

In the late 1860's and early 1870's Apache atrocities mounted to a climax of terror and bloodshed. The scattered outposts of the United States Army were powerless against the wily and sagacious red general and his ruthless warriors. They struck again and again in surprise attacks, and retreated to their impregnable strongholds in the Chiricahuas and Dragoons before soldiers could be organized to pursue them over miles of rough empty desert country. Arizona's Indian troubles finally became a national problem.

In 1872 President Grant sent Major General Oliver O. Howard as a special commissioner to treat with Cochise and to make peace if possible. After four months of negotiations, the General met the chief in his Dragoon Mountain stronghold, and spent ten days there with him unarmed and with only one white companion. This was Thomas L. Jeffords, who conducted him there and was the sole American with whom Cochise was on friendly terms. Called *Tagliato,* the Red Beard, by the Apaches, this remarkable frontiersman and the chief became spiritual brothers through mingling and quaffing each other's blood. The last day of the meeting the Indians held a solemn ceremony for guidance from the Great Spirit. The signs were favorable, and Cochise announced the decision of the Chiricahua Apaches.

"Hereafter, the White Man and the Indian are to drink the same water, eat the same bread, and be at peace."

Cochise kept his end of the bargain to the letter until his death two years later. But other Americans came and broke their word. Indians and white men once more became bitter enemies. However, the story of the great chief Cochise is one of the epics of the Southwest. It will endure like the mighty, upstanding rocks of his homeland as long as men admire courage, character, and integrity.

16 *Buried Treasure*

I'm a thoroughgoing skeptic about buried treasure. The Far West is supposedly honeycombed with fabulous fortunes put in the ground for safe keeping during the past three centuries by the Spaniards, Mexicans, the pioneers, and other assorted characters, good and bad. All one has to do is to run down the correct maps, old records, and cryptic codes which pinpoint the location of the loot, go there and dig it up. There are even buried treasure clubs whose members avidly follow clues wherever they may lead. But I have yet to hear of anybody actually finding one of these holes in the ground, with or without yield.

The Chiricahua Mountains are the site of a famous and much sought-after cache of buried treasure. Some years ago I wrote an article about it for *Desert Magazine*, which was also reprinted in *True West*. For months I received letters from treasure hunters in all parts of the country asking for further information and proposing lucrative partnerships. Inasmuch as some three million dollars is involved, the widespread interest in the whereabouts of the cache can be well understood.

The Buried Treasure of the Chiricahuas is more than a local tall tale. Some points in the story are known facts, and many people are convinced there is evidence the treasure exists. A dying bandit even left a partial inventory of the loot. There was, he said, a cigar box full of diamonds worth one million dollars stolen from a bank vault in Monterrey, Mexico. There were thirty-nine bars of gold bullion valued at six hundred thousand dollars, scores of silver ingots cast in Mexico, ninety thousand Mexican gold dollars, and countless sacks of gold and silver coins. Most interesting, but hardest to believe, the bandit listed two life-sized statues of pure gold—one of the Savior and the other of the Virgin Mary—which once occupied sanctuary niches in a great Mexican cathedral.

The story begins in 1881 at Galeyville, then the unsavory hangout of hold-up men, gun-fighters, rustlers, crooked gamblers, and cutthroats. Rulers of this robbers' roost were Curley Bill Brocius and his lieutenant, John Ringo. Although primarily a cattle thief, Curley Bill, followed by his private army of bully-boys, had numerous ways of augmenting his income without working for it. One of his favorite methods was to waylay Mexican smugglers en route to Tucson. Curley Bill's richest haul of smuggled pelf was made July 1881 in Skeleton Canyon, just across the New Mexico line. The bandits split seventy-five thousand dollars in silver over the dead bodies of slaughtered mules and hapless Mexicans. It is told that they spent every cent of it in four weeks at the bars and gambling tables of Galeyville.

Soon afterwards Curley Bill's grapevine informed him that Mexican smugglers planned to bring in a cargo which far surpassed anything they had handled before. Curley Bill immediately dispatched henchman Jim Hughes to Sonora to scout out the land and get the details. Hughes, a swarthy half-Mexican who spoke Spanish like a native, quickly made friends in Mexico by damning everything gringo from the Constitution to Curley Bill himself.

After many friendly rounds of tequilas, Hughes learned that the smugglers planned to pass through Skeleton Canyon and San Simon Valley in August, following practically the same route as the last pack train. Bursting with the big news, he hurried back to Galeyville, but Curley Bill wasn't there, and nobody knew when he would return.

There was no time to lose, so Jim Hughes decided to pull a magnificent double cross and do the job himself. Zwing Hunt, a mule skinner who aspired to higher things, and a nineteen-year-old embryo desperado named Billy Grounds joined Hughes. He persuaded five other prominent Galeyville citizens to take part. One starry August night the eight of them rode out of the Chiricahuas and headed southeast across San Simon Valley to Skeleton Canyon.

Next morning the Mexican pack train with fifteen men and twice as many mules came winding up the trail over the Peloncillo Mountains. The smugglers were cautious. Under peaked sombreros their eyes constantly scanned the cliffs as they passed down Skeleton Canyon, guns cocked and ready. Near the canyon's lower entrance the fifteen men stopped for tortillas, frijoles, and a siesta before tackling the long, hot trek through the valley. They posted guards up and down the canyon, then stretched out comfortably on the grass under a big oak. Suddenly a fusillade of rifle fire burst from the rocky walls above, and the quiet canyon exploded in a roar of crashing echoes. Three Mexicans lay dead; panic seized the others.

The camp became a wildly confused scramble of shouting, running men, rearing horses, and stampeding mules. The smugglers jumped on their ponies and galloped down the canyon, bullets whistling after them. Three more Mexicans fell as they fled. The heavily laden mules, plunging and kicking in fright, scattered in all directions. During the fray Zwing Hunt was winged by a smuggler's bullet and Billy Grounds bound the wound with his undershirt.

When they rejoined the others they found the problem of what to do with the loot almost unsurmountable. Dead mules were strewn far out into the valley. With no wagons or pack animals the bandits couldn't move the treasure, so it was decided to bury it temporarily at the mouth of the canyon. Two men started digging a hole in the ground beneath three oak trees, while the others rifled the dead mules' aparejos and carried the gold and silver bars and sacks of coins to the hiding place. For many years afterwards gold and silver coins and the bleaching bones of men and mules lined the canyon, and cowboys from neighboring ranches picked up human skulls to use for soap dishes and ash trays.

Jim Hughes, having engineered the raid without the knowledge of Curley Bill, was obliged to return to Galeyville and pretend nothing had happened. The task of moving the loot was entrusted to Zwing Hunt and Billy Grounds. They did this several days later, using a Mexican teamster's four-horse wagon. They buried the loot in a remote spot, killed the Mexican to seal his lips, shot the horses, and used the wagon as a funeral pyre.

Hughes trusted his two companions in crime and waited at Galeyville for their report. It never came. A few days later Hunt and

Grounds met some other outlaws and were beaten to the draw. The younger lad's promising career in banditry was snuffed out, and Hunt was taken to the Tombstone hospital, badly wounded. There, double-crossing Jim Hughes was double-crossed himself, for when he came to call, Hunt escaped by a rear window.

A week or so later, Zwing Hunt's brother reported the wounded bandit had been killed by Apaches, and showed a fresh grave to prove it. That should have ended the story, for Hunt was the only man left who knew the location of the buried treasure. But the rumor of his death was undoubtedly a deliberate subterfuge to throw Jim Hughes off the scent. After some months Zwing Hunt miraculously reappeared, risen from the dead, in his old home town of San Antonio, Texas. His wound was bad and the doctors told him he hadn't long to live. He called his uncle to his bedside and poured out the whole story of the buried treasure. He then drew a map, and died. No one was now alive who had seen the loot, but Hunt's description is detailed and clear.

He explained, and showed on his map, that the cache is located at the foot of Davis Mountain. To the east stretch open plains, and from the summit of the peak a good-sized slice of New Mexico is visible. A mile and a half west a canyon, hemmed in on the far side by wooded hills, cuts the terrain. Through this canyon a stream flows over a ledge in a ten-foot cascade. Hunt said that he and Billy Grounds took a bath under the waterfall after they had buried the treasure. He also put on the map the location of two springs about a mile and a quarter apart, calling the northern one Silver Spring and the other, Gum Spring. He carefully described how to find the exact spot where the loot was buried. It was between the two springs, but a little nearer Silver. The place was marked by a square-sided stone one foot thick and three feet high. On the east face of the stone Hunt had chiseled two crosses, one above the other. Walk twenty paces east, he said, and there is the buried treasure of the Chiricahuas.

This sounds simple enough. Yet of the scores of searchers who have scoured the country in the past eighty years not one has discovered the secret of Zwing Hunt and Billy Grounds.

The principal reason is that nobody ever heard of Davis Moun-

tain, and Hunt neglected to tell where it is. He named the peak after a friend of his whom he and Billy Grounds had buried. There are at least a hundred mountains from which one can look into New Mexico. There are dozens of curving canyons. Charred wood, skeletons, square-sided rocks, and springs a mile and a quarter apart are everywhere. First to try to find the treasure was Hunt's uncle; then Hunt's brother spent thirty-five years combing the hills in vain.

One of the most persistent searchers was Bill Sanders, who had a ranch in the Chiricahuas on West Turkey Creek. Sanders Peak, a prominent pointed summit visible from Painted Canyon Ranch,

Harris Mountain near which,
many believe, Zwing Hunt bur-
ied the fabulous loot.

is named for him. He believed that Zwing Hunt was confused and instead of Davis Mountain, he meant Harris Mountain. The various versions of Hunt's map which have turned up from time to time seem to show that Bill Sanders was right and most recent treasure hunters accept Harris Mountain as a focal point for their quest. Even Phyllis and I have moseyed around that vicinity.

This rather shapeless limestone hump, 5,649 feet in elevation, is an eastern outlier of the Chiricahuas, five miles northwest of Portal. In many respects the surroundings fit Hunt's description. Wide San Simon Valley stretches away to the east, and from the mountain's top it is possible to see into New Mexico. At the foot is a grave. A mile and a half southwest East Turkey Creek Canyon makes a curve, with wooded hills beyond: after rains a stream flows there. A burned wagon was once found nearby.

But there are baffling and conflicting exceptions. The grave contains the remains of a man named Harris, his wife and child, all killed by Apaches. There is no ledge in the canyon to make a ten-foot waterfall, and no one yet has found Gum and Silver Springs, let alone the chiseled, square-sided rock. However, nothing discourages miners, prospectors, or treasure hunters. Year after year the search goes on, and hundreds of tons of Arizona soil are dug up in the everlasting hope that the next shovelful will uncover the fabulous wealth.

As for Phyllis and me, although we lived within ten miles of Harris Mountain, we had no interest in the $3,000,000. My own attitude was solely that of a dedicated historian, who was fired with zeal to separate the wheat from the chaff and to set down the true facts. So it's understandable why I raced over to Animas Valley the minute I heard of an old Mexican there who was reported to have been one of the nine smugglers who escaped Jim Hughes' hijacking foray in 1881. One hundred and two, they said he was. The rumor hinted that he knew more about the treasure than he had told. Well, he still does, as far as I am concerned.

When I got my breath, I accosted the old man on the subject.

He looked up into the sky with eyes of infinite sadness.

"*Chili! Chili!*" he cackled in a rasping voice. "*Tamale y tacos siempre la tortilla. Madre de Dios enchilada.*"

Or at least it sounded something like that. This was all he would say. So he, too, will die with the secret—if he has one—locked in his heart.

17 Heaven Must Wait

The agaves on the sidehill across the road from the Painted Canyon Ranch interested me. Agaves are notable and distinctive citizens of the plant world, not only botanically, but historically, ethnologically, economically, and alcoholically, as well. There are more than three hundred species growing naturally from Colombia to Utah, and on some Caribbean islands, so even their friends have difficulty telling them apart. The Spaniards introduced agaves into Europe during the late fifteen hundreds, and they are now found in the Mediterranean countries, South Africa, India, and Ceylon. I'm not sure what kind we had, but they probably were *americana, atrovirens,* or maybe *palmeri.*

The name agave, pronounced *ah-gah'-vay,* comes from the Greek word *agouos,* meaning admirable. Other names are maguey, mescal, and century plant—the last on the mistaken assumption that it grows for a hundred years, then flowers and dies. Actually the life span of the various species range from seven to thirty years. Until its dramatic bloom of death, the plant consists of a rosette of wickedly spiked, green, pulpy leaves with leathery skins, three to seven feet long. When its time has come, the agave puts up a single stalk from the center of the rosette. Sometimes reaching heights of twenty to twenty-five feet, the upper parts of these slender stems carry candelabra-like panicles of bright yellow, orange, or claret-colored blossoms. They last for a few weeks, and the show is over forever.

Since prehistoric times the agave has been one of the most important plants in Mexico and the Southwest. The Indians made soap from the roots, ate roasted agave stems, chewed them raw as a delicacy, and got drunk on the fermented sap. Pulque, the national alcoholic drink of Mexico, is distilled from the maguey, as are mescal and mescal de tequila. The maguey is the source of sisal

Blossoming agave.

hemp, one of Mexico's big industries, and different species of agaves furnish fibers for rope, cordage, bagging, brushes, and baskets. Besides all these useful attributes, the agaves are decorative and widely planted for purely ornamental purposes. Total abstainers may object to the derivation of the agave's name, but "admirable" seems to be an apt adjective to describe a plant which showers its serious and light-hearted beneficences in so many directions.

Each spring a few of our agaves sprouted their stems, then blossomed, and expired. The stalks shot up with such amazing rapidity that I decided to measure their daily growth. I selected an agave that was starting an especially lusty stalk and went up the hill each afternoon with a twenty-foot pole, pocket tape, and pencil. My markings on the pole recorded an upward surge of more than three feet a day at the beginning, later slowing down to around ten inches every twenty-four hours. My pole wasn't long enough, and I had to use an extension, as the stalk topped out at twenty-two feet before it stopped and burst into bloom.

One afternoon as I was engaged in my absorbing agave field

My pole wasn't long enough.

project, Beautiful stopped watching me and broke into her high-pitched bark which she reserved for welcoming visitors. I turned to see a man climbing up the steep hillside. He introduced himself as Dr. Mont A. Cazier, at that time Chairman of the Department of Insects and Spiders at New York's American Museum of Natural History. Phyllis had told him where to find me.

"Is your place for sale?" he asked.

This took me completely by surprise. "Why, I don't know," I stammered. "We've never thought about it."

"It would make an ideal site for our Southwestern Research Station," said Dr. Cazier.

"Let's talk it over," I suggested, and we went down the slope to the house.

On the way he asked me what we would want for the ranch, if we did sell. This struck me as a purely academic question, but I mentally reached into the air, found a price, and named it. I later discovered that he had asked Phyllis the same thing and received a different quotation. My wife is noted for her generosity, and it was considerably lower than mine.

We were drinking tequila sours that spring in honor of our agaves. I don't now remember if Dr. Cazier indulged, but Phyllis's *Playa del Mar* blend is cool and refreshing, and I was ready for a round or two after my labors on the hill. At any rate, we three sat on the screened porch and discussed the unexpected proposition.

Dr. Cazier had a mission and as he talked an apostolic zeal lighted his eyes. He explained that after several years of intensive search he had come to the conclusion the Chiricahua Mountains were the best location in the Southwest for a field station of the American Museum. He was convinced that our ranch would make perfect headquarters for scientific studies in practically all phases of Southwestern natural history. He visualized a center with year-round facilities available to qualified researchers in a dozen branches of science.

"It can't be touched anywhere," said Dr. Cazier. "Everyone I've talked with agrees that this is the logical place for biological field work. There is probably more natural history within eighteen miles of where we're sitting than anywhere else in the world."

Of this, of course, we were fully aware. But it was an uncommon switch for a prospective buyer to tell the sellers theirs is the most superior piece of property that can be found. It warmed us to this ardent entomologist. In fact, Dr. Cazier has a persuasive personality, and the very boldness and sweep of his plan fired our imaginations. So we showed him around the place, and bade him farewell in a sort of dream-like daze.

After watching his carry-all disappear down the road, we looked at each other. All I could say was, "I'll be darned!" Phyllis was more articulate.

"I'll never sell Painted Canyon," she said emphatically. "Never! Never!"

Although we hadn't spoken of it, I think both of us assumed we would live out the rest of our days in the Chiricahuas. Even the thought of living anywhere else came as a jolting shock. For never again could we find such congenial surroundings. Each day was a fresh and rewarding experience which we greeted with pleasurable anticipation. At Painted Canyon it was good just to be alive. However, in this world for every plus there is a minus, so we brewed a pot of coffee, sat down, and balanced the pros against the cons.

Of one thing we were certain—neither of us had yearned for cosmopolitan amenities. If we lacked culture and sophistication, we were happy that way. A-go-go, the jet set, and to be "where the action is" had no appeal whatever. Nor did we miss the theatre, concerts, lectures, libraries, and clubs. As for art, we considered it superfluous to view other people's interpretations of Nature and Man. We were exposed to some of the finest examples of both and were used to forming our own first-hand impressions. Around us on all sides was the superb artistry of Nature with an infinite variety of form and color, which constantly changed from hour to hour, even minute to minute. Phyllis and I looked up at the cliffs glowing golden in the afternoon sunlight.

No, we agreed, we wouldn't sell.

On the other hand, we had chosen full-time professional writing as a career. There was no question that the remoteness of Painted Canyon Ranch was a handicap in our work. As free-lance writers

The artistry of nature.

we were increasingly out of touch with editors, publishers, and markets. Phyllis was conducting a fast-growing literary counselling service, and we held several writing courses, one of which required three hundred miles round-trip driving each meeting. Then, too, we were co-directors of the Southwest Writers' Workshop and Conference at Northern Arizona University in Flagstaff. This meant more than two weeks' absence from home each summer.

Well, maybe we ought to accept Dr. Cazier's offer. "What do you think?" we asked each other.

Both of us agreed that Painted Canyon Ranch provided an inspirational environment for a novelist or one whose stories emerge full-fledged from the top of his head. But Phyllis and I, unfortunately, are not creative writers. My specialties are travel, exploration, human events, history, and natural history among the mountains, forests, and deserts of the Far West. I am a guide rather than an interpreter, a roving reporter not an analyst. My aim is to describe examples of our superb natural and human heritage in the hope that some of my enthusiasm will rub off on the reader. There is, I fondly believe, a place for a mere water carrier as well as the in-depth philosopher. But this kind of writing takes research, legwork, and considerable travel. My territory covers eleven large states, and I found that the Chiricahuas were poorly situated for articles on places in northern Utah, the Montana Rockies, or the Pacific Northwest.

Yes, Phyllis and I concluded we would sell Painted Canyon Ranch.

Our heads told us it was the right thing to do, but our hearts never quite forgave us for abandoning this sky island retreat in the Chiricahuas.

When we told our friends, most of them were flabbergasted. "You don't mean that you're going to give up this heaven on earth?" they exclaimed incredulously.

"Heaven must wait," was my usual answer to this, but whatever I said, I knew they wouldn't understand.

However, we soon discovered the move wasn't imminent. After Dr. Cazier's departure for New York, there followed an unreal twilight period of over a year while negotiations were in progress.

We still legally owned Painted Canyon Ranch, but actually we shared it with the American Museum of Natural History. A representative, his wife, and the museum architect stayed with us for a time, probing, delving, inspecting, taking measurements, and making plans. Then when we were absent at the Writers' Conference that summer, Dr. Cazier and a couple of caretakers took over the ranch. When we returned two eminent scientists were having a learned discussion on plant rust in the living room. Both ignored us, and we felt more like intruders than hosts. There were also constant long-distance phone calls from New York and an endless two-way stream of air-mail letters. It is doubtful if a buyer ever sam-

Heaven must wait!

pled, checked, and analyzed his contemplated purchase more thoroughly.

Word finally came that amateur entomologist David Rockefeller had agreed to present the Painted Canyon Ranch to the Museum for a research station if Dr. Cazier could raise running expenses for ten years. Also individuals and organizations pledged contributions, one donor promising funds to construct a fully equipped modern biological laboratory on the premises. Meanwhile Phyllis and I were busy making our own plans for the future. Although we had the whole world to choose from, we elected to stay in our favorite part of it and bought a house in Tucson. How

urban life would affect us humans, Beautiful, and the cats we didn't know, but Arizona's second largest center of population offers quick access to the mountains and deserts we loved so well.

It was the April following Dr. Cazier's first visit when the final documents were signed and the deal consummated. Presumably there wasn't a moment to lose, for the new proprietor notified us he was arriving that afternoon. He did, his carry-all loaded with nourishing staples for the scientists. It was up to us to get out—fast. Gorgeous, a ranch fixture, and the chickens were included in the sale; Mamie and the rabbits found a good home with the Hoskins. However, our immediate departure was somewhat complicated by an invitation to a farewell dinner with friends in Portal. So we rounded up Pinky and Whitey, and closed them in the dining room. There wasn't a sign of Barney. We hunted and we called, whistled and shouted within a quarter-mile radius of the house—but no cat.

We had to leave for our engagement. "We'll pick him up when we get back," Phyllis and I assured each other. But underneath both of us were worried.

On our return Barney was still missing. It was pitch dark, and we repeated our search and cajoling by flashlight without results. Finally we gave up—it was nine o'clock, and we had a hundred-and-fifty-mile drive ahead of us.

"We'll be down and get Barney as soon as possible," I said to Dr. Cazier. "Take good care of him, he's one of the family."

Phyllis and I loaded the station wagon, put Pinky and Whitey in two of the three "cat pullmans" we'd rented in Tucson, Beautiful jumped in the back seat, and we were ready for the take-off. But not quite. A soft *meow* sounded, and out of the blackness stalked Barney with deliberate, unhurried tread. It seems a bit foolish the relief Phyllis and I felt. We happily put the errant cat in his box, said good-bye to Dr. Cazier, and wished him good luck. Then we drove off down the road into the night.

Three hours later as we turned the key and opened the front door of our new home, the grandfather's clock in the living room greeted us with its familiar chimes, then struck twelve.

Another day had begun.

Acknowledgments

The author has written many articles on the Chiricahua Mountains and other southeastern Arizona "sky islands." He wishes to thank the editors of the following publications for permission to use excerpts and anecdotes from his previous writings: *Arizona Highways, Audubon, Desert* for the buried treasure story, *Natural History* and *Nature, Pacific Discovery* for parts of "High Country" and "Land of Standing Rocks," and *Westways*.

DATE DUE